Daphne du Maurier,
Haunted Heiress

Personal Takes

*A*n occasional series of short books,
in which noted critics write about the
persistent hold particular writers,
artists, or cultural phenomena have
had on their imaginations.

Daphne du Maurier,
Haunted Heiress

Nina Auerbach

PENN

University of Pennsylvania Press
Philadelphia

Copyright © 2000 University of Pennsylvania Press
Printed in the United States of America on acid-free paper

10 9 8 7 6 5 4 3 2 1

Published by
University of Pennsylvania Press
Philadelphia, Pennsylvania 19104-4011

Library of Congress Cataloging-in-Publication Data

Auerbach, Nina, 1943–
    Daphne du Maurier, haunted heiress / Nina Auerbach.
        p.   cm. — (Personal takes)
    Includes bibliographical references (p.   ) and index.
    ISBN 0-8122-3530-4 (alk. paper)
        1. Du Maurier, Daphne, Dame, 1907–   2. Du Maurier, Daphne,
Dame, 1907–   —Family. 3. Du Maurier, Daphne, Dame, 1907–   —Psychology.
4. Women novelists, English—20th century—Family relationships. 5. Psychological
fiction, English—History and criticism. 6. Women novelists, English—
20th century Biography. 7. Du Maurier, Gerald, Sir, 1873–1934—Influence.
8. Du Maurier, George, 1834–1896—Influence. 9. Fathers and daughters—Great
Britain. 10. Grandfathers—Great Britain. 11. Du Maurier family.
I. Title. II. Series.
PR6007.U47Z55 1999
823' .912—dc21
[B]   99–34174
                                                                        CIP

For Carolyn Heilbrun

~

Contents

1

Reading Furtively, by Flashlight

All books seem better when I'm not supposed to be reading them. I never should read Daphne du Maurier, but I regularly do.

I don't read her nicknames or titles. When she married, her family cutely called her "Bing"; after she and her husband were dignified by royalty, she became "Lady Browning, D.B.E.," or, in card catalogues and on official occasions, *Dame* Daphne du Maurier.

I don't read the family pet or the Dame, and above all, I don't read "the author of *Rebecca*," a label that confined du Maurier from the publication of that novel early in her career, in 1938, up to and beyond her death, in 1989. I didn't read *Rebecca* until late in my furtive encounters with the author of sixteen other novels, six biographies, four books of articles and memoirs, two plays, and eight collections of stories. Most of the novels were bestsellers; the biographies and stories are startlingly brilliant; but for most people, du Maurier remains "the author of *Rebecca*."

Rebecca is a grim anatomy of wifehood. Rebecca, the dead, bad wife, exists only as a hovering name; the good second wife, who tells the story, has no name and little energy. Most du Maurier narrators are full of anger and activity, traits she considered masculine, so she made them men, but her fascinating, passionate, sardonic male-centered novels are forgotten. As I write, *Rebecca*, masochistic, derivative, and only quasi-coherent—unlike almost all her other works—is the only Daphne du Maurier novel in print. One reason I remain loyal to this strange writer and unlikable woman is the injustice of her label as a writer of escapist women's romance. Having read just about everything she wrote, I can imagine that I alone know the difficult, resentful author who fought against the dear, familiar presence she became in the eyes of the world.

When I first discovered Daphne du Maurier, I was twelve, and I avoided *Rebecca*, not out of high principle, but because I don't think they had it in Portland, Maine, the nearest civilized center to my isolated summer camp. I wasn't supposed to read Daphne du Maurier in camp because we weren't supposed to read anything, at least not with persistence or ferocity: in 1955, we were supposed to play team sports, hike, and get along with each other, all of which I did my best to resist. Every two weeks or so, counselors would load us on the truck and take us to Portland; on the way, we were supposed to sing camp songs very loudly; once there, we would eat ice cream, ride a sad little Ferris wheel, and get back on the truck.

But I was wicked: I bought books at a local drugstore. The selection was not great, and the few books on its rack were scarcely fit for girls at camp. I remember finding *The Lost Weekend* there, a clinical account of alcoholism that was a good escape from heartiness. Somewhere in the middle of the summer I found Daphne du Maurier. Her euphonious, hybrid name lured me immediately, long before I knew its history: it seemed created to charm and to mystify. Even in that dusty drugstore, *Rebecca* would have been obsolete by 1955, but they did have some of her works from the 1940s: *The King's General* (1946) and *Hungry Hill* (1943).

Oddly, two more recent novels, *The Parasites* (1949) and *My Cousin Rachel* (1951), hadn't reached Portland, or they were long sold out. I read neither of these until I was an adult, but I would have adored both when I was twelve. *The Parasites*, an account of a beautiful, heartless theatrical family, would have reinforced my personal mythology of specialness; the more famous *My Cousin Rachel*, a story of a perfect woman impaled on the narrative of the men she torments, would have intensified my budding irony and paranoia. *The Parasites* and *My Cousin Rachel* are wry, sophisticated accounts of superior spirits, not far from the less urbane Salinger novels we were reading avidly at the same time. *The King's General* and *Hungry Hill*, the novels that happened to be in Portland's drugstore, were historical. The Daphne du Maurier who is entwined in her dream of history is still the one who fascinates me.

It turns out that I began with minor du Maurier; these uncharacteristic historical novels mesh uneasily with her private landscape. Like many of us, Daphne du Maurier had difficulty imagining any world she hadn't lived in, though she saw worlds she never lived in as her own. Nevertheless, the two novels at the Portland drugstore—especially the little-known *Hungry Hill*—introduced me to a woman wrestling with an imagined past, both national and familial. That past is not meticulously reconstructed; it is an entity, a dream, that feeds on the present and sometimes irradiates it. (The wistful narrator of *The Scapegoat* strolls through Orléans possessed by visions of praying with Joan of Arc, "watching my half-boy with her pure, fanatic's eyes"—a dream that will in a sense come true in the course of his story.)[1] When I grew up to become a specialist in Victorian England, I was similarly haunted by a dream past that would neither include me nor go away.

But in camp, I knew nothing about Daphne du Maurier beyond the fact that she was glorious flashlight reading: when everything was quiet and dark, after the bugle had wailed out "Taps" and the counselors had gone off to their special hut to complain about us and, we assumed, to talk about sex, and my bunkmates had put their bite plates in and set their hair and were snoring and churning in their sleep, I extracted my flashlight, the one I was supposed to use for camping out, and curled up surreptitiously with *Hungry Hill*. (*The*

King's General, though more romantic, was less enticing: this long account of the English Civil War seemed confused and confusing to me, as it still does.) *Hungry Hill*, bleak and lugubrious, made superb forbidden reading as unknown animals chirped and prowled outside the bunk in which I was supposed to be healthily asleep.

Technically, there was nothing subversive about *Hungry Hill* as subversion was defined in 1955: like most of Daphne du Maurier's novels, it had no sex and not much credible love. It did have politics, but these were remote and feudal, not the sort of questioning that was getting Americans in trouble with congressional committees. What riveted me, I think, was the century-long evolution of an Irish family from a Victorian past to a war-ravaged present: the novel begins in 1820, when an enterprising capitalist, "Copper" John Brodrick, digs a copper mine in ancient Hungry Hill; it ends during the Irish Rebellion in 1920 with the closing of the mine and the dispossession of Copper John's great-great-grandson.

I thought I loved the book because it was sad: each generation of heirs slips farther from the ruthless stature of Copper John, failing to govern not only the mine but also Clonmere, the family estate. Their decline is fated, for at the beginning, a member of a rival family, the disreputable, gypsylike Donovans, curses Copper John and "not only you, but your son after you, and your grandsons, and may your wealth bring them nothing but despair and desolation and evil, until the last of them stands humble and ashamed amongst the ruin of it, with the Donovans back again in Clonmere in the land that belongs to them."[2] The curse is, of course, fulfilled at the end, but while it gave me an excuse to be sad, I think I read *Hungry Hill* so avidly by flashlight because of the incompetence of Brodrick after Brodrick. I was fascinated, even wickedly delighted, by the spectacle of these enfeebled, privileged men, and I think Daphne du Maurier was too.

Despite the fame of the female-centered *Rebecca*, *Hungry Hill*, like Daphne du Maurier's best, most characteristic novels, is dominated by powerful men: women are there to torment, to soothe, to prop up men and cover up for them, to die conveniently or inconveniently. Each Brodrick generation has a Henry—who is always charming, affable, and weak—and a John, who is always brooding, unstable, and self-destructive. Two generations of Johns and Henrys fall in love with the same woman, a device du Maurier uses to blur the boundaries between those unstable entities she calls men. Since the last male of the line is named John-Henry, he should synthesize the warring fraternal elements, but he does so only to complete the Brodricks' dispossession, handing over the ruins of Clonmere, along with his last three pounds, to a rapacious Donovan.

My favorite chapters concerned, not the mine, but the estate, Clonmere. Spanning 1837-1895—coincidentally, the peak Victorian years I would later study as avidly as I had read *Hungry Hill*—they deal with the loss of the estate under the care of the third generation, the grandsons of Copper John. "Wild Johnnie," the maddest John, and his brother, the most lovable, but also, it turns out, the weakest Henry, epitomize the family and destroy it.

Spoiled by his adoring mother, prone to rages, obsessed all his life with inheriting Clonmere, Wild Johnnie is lured into alcoholism and debauchery by the scheming Donovans, who always lurk on the sidelines to prey on Brodrick weaknesses. When Copper John finally dies and Johnnie moves into Clonmere, he doesn't know what to do with it. The servants and villagers shun him, wishing he were his charming younger brother Henry. Through his own weaknesses and the wiles of the Donovans, he becomes an exile and a suicide.

For me, at least, Wild Johnnie, paralyzed by his inheritance, is a more compelling figure than the wife in *Rebecca* who shrinks before Manderley, for Johnnie is no shy interloper, but the legitimate heir. Throughout Daphne du Maurier's novels, the falls of men are more compelling than those of women because her men have everything to lose; while women are humble by definition, men embody power and privilege. In their magnitude, they are like heroes of Greek tragedy, but their heroism is a posture: we know them so well that we share their embarrassed ineptitude in their role. Wild Johnnie's helplessness seemed harrowing—and also exhilarating—to me in 1955, and it does still.

It is not renegade Johnnie, however, but his beloved brother Henry, the ideal lord of the manor, who loses the estate. Johnnie is paralyzed by Henry's perfection and by hopeless love for Henry's perfect, motherly wife; but when this shining couple moves into Clonmere after Johnnie's death, Henry proves a counterfeit image of rule. When his angel-wife dies in childbirth, his will dissipates as his brother's had; he falls prey to an imperious English widow who hates Clonmere and the Brodrick children. She moves Henry to London and dispossesses his heir. The next Henry, lost, drifts around Canada, returning to live in the village and becoming a clerk in the failing family mine until his father sells the mine and the Donovans kill this final, exhausted heir.

Somehow this saga about the loss of an estate pulverized me when I was twelve. Was it because I had never known estates existed? What drew me to that very British symbol of continuity and command? (*Hungry Hill* is ostensibly Irish, but it has no Irish flavor, functioning, like all Daphne du Maurier's countries, as a parable of English decay.) As an American, I had always assumed that every generation started life over again in a new beginning: I was stricken by the tragedy of the recurrent Johns and Henrys, each a diluted version of the last, all disintegrating under the inheritance that is their only identity.

When I was not gripped by the spectacle of loss and decline, I looked, out of the corner of my eye, at the women in the saga. They are an apparently subservient group. None is independent of the men's plots; all are obliquely perceived as functions of John's or Henry's destinies; but all, even the good women, are more vividly self-reliant than the powerful passive Brodricks they inadvertently destroy.

I had never encountered female characters like these. The most striking one is Fanny-Rosa, perpetually called "elusive," not because she is shadowy or silent, but because there is so much more of her than her story allows. Beautiful, sexy, daring, and lower class (one character suggests snobbishly, and inaccurately, that her proletarian blood caused the fall of the Brodricks), Fanny-Rosa marries an earlier John who lives only to adore her. When, characteristically, he sinks into domestic bliss and helpless passivity, she runs the estate while raising their five children. Eccentric slob, wise wife, and expert chatelaine, she is abandoned by her sons. Her adored Johnnie throws her out of Clonmere in a fit of drunken despair; supposedly gentle Henry lets his English fiancée institutionalize the abandoned Fanny-Rosa, who is now a compulsive gambler, in a "nice" rest home in Nice.

Fanny-Rosa is a typical Daphne du Maurier woman: she is neither feminist nor rebel (du Maurier infallibly certifies those spunky women she does approve of by making them want to be boys). She does woman's work but she spills out all over her role, spoiling the men who ultimately victimize her. This inadvertent (indeed, well-meaning) ability to ruin men introduced me to a new dimension of relationships: men were so fragile that even good women could sap their will. Perhaps this domestic draining reinforced my growing attraction to vampires, but Fanny-Rosa does not think of herself as a vampire. She does her domestic duty.

Hungry Hill is suggestive about women, but like Daphne du Maurier herself, I was most interested in its men and the worlds they possess. Feudal patriarchy was clearly inequitable and unworkable, but it did produce a more far-reaching family, and thus a more interesting one, than the isolated units that were supposed to be blissful in the 1950s. The Brodricks encompass estate, village, and mine: their family is not a haven but a dynasty. For me, a family was an enclosure to reach beyond—even then, I did not want to live the way my family lived, and I assumed I wouldn't have to—but for the Brodricks, "family" is an expansive world of privilege and possession. For me, as a mid-century American woman, the world lay beyond family life, while for the Brodricks, losing family means losing the world. Rebellion is dispossession. This seemed to me, and still does, a deeply poignant dilemma, one that pervades Daphne du Maurier's career.

Because *Hungry Hill* is so English (though in Irish guise), so steeped in inheritance and tradition, it gave me my first glimmer of different ways to order the world. It was not that I wanted Clonmere; neither did the Brodricks who coveted it and could not live there. As an American, I had no idea that a Clonmere, giving weight and perpetuity to a name, existed to be lost. True, there was Tara in *Gone with the Wind*, but Tara was in its first generation when it fell from estatehood. An American estate lived only a lifetime; an English (or Irish) estate was a bond with the past. Clonmere is an elitist conception, a symbol of unjust grandeur more oppressive than welcoming, but for me it was a tantalizingly un-American home to yearn for and to lose. Sharing a dingy camp cabin with a gaggle of girls and their chewing gum and braces, I thought I deserved Clonmere if the Brodricks didn't.

Apart from my burgeoning snobbery, I felt as if I knew the Brodricks. True, all were pattern Johns or Henrys, but each had his own way of seeing the world, his own surprising means of living his destiny. Among literary critics, it has long been unfashionable to praise fictional characters as lifelike—in their vividness and roundedness, their peculiar way of seeing as well as being seen, their capacity to surprise—but Daphne du Maurier's male characters are lifelike. For her, history was people, and people were men. She was as adept at becoming someone else as the actor-father she adored and scrutinized; she was uncannily deft at becoming men, those envied and defective others. Readers who know her only through her female-centered romances—*Rebecca, Jamaica Inn,* and *Frenchman's Creek*—imagine her males as inflated fantasy figures, but the men in these romances exist primarily to characterize the confined woman who sees them. In *Hungry Hill,* and her many other novels in which men exist on their own terms, as their own centers of consciousness, the reader eavesdrops on a forbidden world of masculinity, privilege, and radical incompetence.

Daphne du Maurier's were not the first men I met, in or out of novels. World War II novels like *From Here to Eternity* and *Battle Cry* were part of my inappropriate summer reading. But their brawny soldiers, strutting or sensitive, seemed more like male impersonations than the men of du Maurier's supposedly domestic fiction. Du Maurier men, not Leon Uris men, seemed like the men I knew, even the damp-palmed boys with whom I danced at camp socials. Daphne du Maurier's uncanny fictional ability to become a man without revering men or making a case against them is utterly unwomanly—some might even call her self-transformations antiwomanly—but I continue to admire du Maurier's audacity in choosing roles beyond her own, roles she plays with sympathetic penetration. Never until I lived with Daphne du Maurier's Brodricks did I believe in the men who strutted and died.

I'm afraid the story of my introduction to Daphne du Maurier exposes me as a trash-reading snob, and I'm afraid I've remained one, though a university English department, if not exactly an estate, became a more appropriate home than a camp bunk for my sense of specialness, my resentment of strictures and boundaries, my good-natured but fundamental unkindness. As writer and (as I learned later) as woman, Daphne du Maurier shares these antisocial qualities and elicits them. She is not a writer who appeals to one's best self. Nor does a very similar novelist, Jane Austen, but Jane Austen has been loved through generations because she knows how to appear ordinary, a lesson the privileged Daphne du Maurier thought she never had to learn.

Camp ended. I grew up a little and read a lot, no longer by flashlight—in high school I read the Russian and Continental novelists, Stendhal, Tolstoy, Dostoevsky, Mann, with a leaven of Salinger and Shirley Jackson—and I met people I liked, with whom I didn't have to share a cabin. By 1958, when I was fifteen, I thought I had a lot of style. I did have a new degree of freedom to prowl around New York, go to the theater, drink cappuccino. If I thought back to *Hungry Hill* at all, I remembered Daphne du Maurier as an escapist writer (a label with which she is still belittled, as if *Hamlet* or *War and Peace* or any great narrative is not escapist). I thought I had grown above her until I read her new novel, *The Scapegoat* (1957), and fell under that spell again.

My experience with Daphne du Maurier has always been the same. I devour her, leave her, and vaguely decide that she has satisfied some immature neurotic need in me that I no longer have. Then some years later I read her again and I fall back into her world. As I write this, she is dead, pigeonholed, and dismissed. I, however, am now an English professor in my fifties with the confidence to affirm that from 1955 to the present, I've read Daphne du Maurier, not because I need a childish escape, but because she's a complex, powerful, unique writer, so unorthodox that no critical tradition, from formalism to feminism, can digest her.

When I read *The Scapegoat*, not only was I out of camp, but it was no longer summer. I read the novel in the fall, I think, during a particularly busy and lively school year. It made no difference. I was hooked and possessed.

It didn't occur to me in 1958, at least not consciously, that *The Scapegoat* is a more successful variation of *Hungry Hill*. *The Scapegoat* is another un-English novel, though its French setting is closer than Ireland to du Maurier's imagination: her grandfather, the artist and novelist George du Maurier, grew up in a France he never ceased to romanticize; for Daphne, her French origins and family name composed one of her many unrealized selves. The appearance of the un-realized self is the theme of *The Scapegoat*—an eminently Victorian idea, though I didn't realize it at the time.

The Scapegoat, like *Hungry Hill*, deals with a man struggling with his role of lord of the manor, ruling family, estate, and firm—not, here, a copper mine, but a straggling, old-fashioned glass foundry. His reign is especially difficult because he is not the man he plays. John, the English narrator, begins the novel in despair over his solitary, vicarious life teaching French. He is traveling through the France of his expertise, a country he is too isolated to understand. Like Robert Louis Stevenson's Dr. Jekyll, he longs to release "the self who clamored for release, the man within," whom he imagines as a careless man, one with "a mocking laugh, a casual heart, a swift-roused temper and a ribald tongue" (p. 6).

Magically, his laughing double appears before him as a French count, Jean de Gué. Eager to escape his many entanglements, Jean tricks John into an exchange of identities. Before he knows it, John is the lord of an ancient château, an acrimonious family, an understanding mistress, and an unprofitable glass foundry.

Why did I find this story of doubling and identity exchange so enthralling? In part, I think, because it complicates the usual Jekyll/

Hyde (or *Tale of Two Cities*) antithesis. The English John is a good man because an empty one; his callous (therefore "bad"?) French counterpart wants to flee his property, especially his female property ("I have too many possessions. Human ones," he explains to the yearning John [p. 18]). But John and Jean are not so much moral opposites as blurred reflections. John puts on Jean's clothes and begins to melt into a new French self, the vibrant "man within" who was there all along. *The Scapegoat* eludes the moralism its form seems to demand. When John encounters his supposed mother, his daughter, his sister, his mistresses, he responds to them as Jean even before he learns the family plot. Jean wants to flee family; John wants to belong; but when the Englishman becomes head of a French estate, he loses his own contours.

Family life in *The Scapegoat* is a wretched affair, at least until it is purged by the authentic scapegoat, who is neither John nor Jean; but it is also strangely dreamlike and theatrical. It was this dreamlike opacity that pulled me into du Maurier's family plot. In the time and country in which I first read *The Scapegoat*, families were by definition intimate, if fraught; from the naturalistic theater of Miller and O'Neill to the Freudian ideology that pervaded supposedly sophisticated New York to the assumption that girls like me wanted only to start another family, family values were the only authentic constituents of identity. *The Scapegoat* was a piquant alternative. Despite John's clumsy befuddlement before the demands of his pseudo-family, he deceives everyone. Only the dogs—and, later, his restful mistress, who is beyond the family circle—recognize the impostor. The women never question the nature of the man they cling to.

For John and Jean, family life is by definition a ruler's game—also a piquant observation in 1958, when questions of power and privilege never penetrated domestic ideals. In an American novel, one written perhaps by a sensitive writer like Carson McCullers, John would find intimacy and understanding in his adoptive family, or at least he would want to; in *The Scapegoat*, he learns to handle power. He unabashedly owns, and learns to control, the women who depend on him. When Jean returns, John has learned his lesson. He equates proprietorship with love: "I was the possessor now, he the intruder. The château was my château, the people were my people, the family who in a few minutes would sit with me round the table were my family, my flesh and blood; they belonged to me and I to them" (p. 300). John becomes a family man when he becomes a possessor. Perhaps I should have been offended by du Maurier's unflinching assumption that family life for men involves wielding power over women's lives, but I found it a refreshing if cold-hearted antidote to American sentimentality.

In the same vein, *The Scapegoat* fascinated me because its women were all so miserable. They were miserable not because they were unloved (or, in the jargon of the day, "unfulfilled") but because they were dependent. In many ways *The Scapegoat* is, like *Hungry Hill* and many of du Maurier's other male-centered novels, an account of women's condition told from an oblique male perspective. As head of the family and estate, John is confronted with a pageant of female misery in Jean's mother, sister, mistresses, wife, and daughter. All are thwarted, demanding, plaintive, possessive, not unlike ordinary middle-class women of the 1950s. Though it reaches nostalgically toward a feudal past, *The Scapegoat* is pitilessly contemporary.

Its newly fledged patriarch is stunned by the absoluteness of his power. Whether or not his family understands him, he can make or unmake their lives: "I could, if I chose, do incalculable harm to these people whom I did not know—injure them, upset their lives, put them at odds with one another—and it would not matter to me because they were dummies, strangers, they had nothing to do with my life" (p. 34). Like the second wife in *Rebecca*, he blunders excruciatingly as he becomes enmeshed in Jean's past perfidies. Miraculously, though, the family is healed by the death of its most wretched member: Jean's sour wife, Françoise, who, toward the end, falls or jumps to her death, releasing the others from their financial, vocational, and emotional burdens. As is so often true in Daphne du Maurier's fiction, the wife is the true scapegoat. As Françoise's eerie daughter, Marie-Noel, puts it: "since Maman died, everyone is getting what they want" (p. 298). What these bitter, sniping women want is work and authority. At the end John has become lordly and loving enough to give it to them.

I fear I sound doctrinaire, and thus false to the intensity of reading. I hear myself claiming that I loved *The Scapegoat* when I was fifteen because it anticipated *The Feminine Mystique* in its analysis of privileged women living useless, helpless lives. Am I approving it after the fact because it anticipated the sort of feminist analysis of gender and power that we now know so well we forget it was once fresh and dangerous? Daphne du Maurier may have been unsentimental about family values, but she had no interest in liberating fifteen-year-old American girls. She saw herself less as a feminist than as a chosen spirit: she had no interest in the sort of collective, class analysis of women's condition that gained acceptance in the early 1970s, when her career was fading. Her realism was, and is, compelling to me because it is inseparable from her alienated magic. I have found in no other writer's work the same tough-minded anatomy of family life combined with so eerie a patina of domestic strangeness.

The family John learns to govern—and thus to love—may lack intimacy, but it is suffused with a mutual mirroring that is terrifying in its ordinariness. Like the recurrent Johns and Henrys in *Hungry Hill*, different generations may not know each other, but they *are* each other. When John first meets his supposed daughter, ardent little Marie-Noel, he sees not affinity but identity. Like his supposed mother, the massive countess who has become a timorous morphine addict, Marie-Noel is a fragment of his double and, hence, of himself: "a replica of Jean de Gué, and therefore in fantastic fashion of a self long buried in the past so forgotten" (p. 57). Later on, the three generations mystically merge. As the addicted countess whines for morphine, "the mask became a face, and the face hers and mine and Marie-Noel's. The three of us were together, looking out at me from her eyes, and the voice was no longer deep and guttural but the voice of the child when she spoke to me the first evening" (p. 210). Though the countess and Marie-Noel have little in common, they are fragments of each other and of a larger, impalpable being. This bizarre mythology of family, in which ancestors remain alive in the living, effecting perpetual transformations, is, as we shall see, the foundation of Daphne du Maurier's obsessively genealogical art.

The family in *The Scapegoat* is distant, ritualized, and haunted by itself. Daphne du Maurier's vision is clinical, but it is also hermetic. Eleven-year-old Marie-Noel looks like a typical child of her decade, quivering with too much intensity for any available life, but in her combination of oedipal adoration and spiritual ambition she becomes the vehicle of a miracle. Marie-Noel begins the novel as the whimsical girl a tender male writer like J. M. Barrie or J. D. Salinger might dream: she ends as an incipient Joan of Arc. Daphne du Maurier is far from devout about her demanding little saint; Marie-Noel may be as close to demons as she is to God; she is certainly more magical than virtuous. In her spiritual ferocity, though, she is neither cute nor a martyr, but the vessel of nonnatural powers that infuse the family in *The Scapegoat* with the allure of inspiration as well as the demon of understanding.

I may not be putting this well. It's easier to explain why one doesn't like something than why one does; but the Daphne du Maurier I kept returning to as a teenager, and keep returning to now, is far from a compliant fulfiller of feminine (or feminist) wishes. Her vision of relationships, especially family relationships, is unapologetically brutal. The magic that runs through her stories does not soften the characters or resolve their tensions, as, for instance, does that magic moment in Charlotte Brontë's *Jane Eyre* when Jane hears Rochester cry out to her from miles away. The supernatural cry in *Jane Eyre* is an affirmation of Jane's "powers," as she calls them, and a cry of reunion; in Daphne du Maurier's novels, and even more baldly in her tales, the powers that erupt at surprising moments in unexpected characters are thwarting symptoms of irresolution. Though critics lazily call du Maurier a descendant of the Brontës, her supernaturalism does not, like theirs, bring the story to rest; it intensifies the frustration underlying her supposed romances.[3] From the 1950s to the present, I was, and remain, enthralled by Daphne du Maurier because of her antiromantic refusal to satisfy predictable desires.

The two novels that drew me to du Maurier are oddly alike. Both are about powerful men with perilously unstable identities; both engulf their protagonists in families fraught with tradition and the threat of obliteration; both take place out of England. With the exception of the last category—in general, Daphne du Maurier is an inveterately English novelist—*Hungry Hill* and *The Scapegoat* typify the boldest, most interesting qualities of du Maurier's vision. When I first read these novels, I never would have thought that forty years later, no one would know them, though as "the author of *Rebecca*" Daphne du Maurier remains a familiar name. I suspect she too would have muttered at the fact that the most audacious of her many selves is the one in oblivion.

When, in preparation for writing this book, I returned to *Hungry Hill* and *The Scapegoat*, the new dimensions I found only intensified their fascination. It was odd to reread *Hungry Hill* after all the years since camp. I had expected it to come flooding back, but in fact I didn't remember a single character or incident: I couldn't even reexperience the accompanying flashlight, camp bunk, mysterious animal noises outside. Still, under different circumstances and as a different self, only a few weeks before my fifty-fifth birthday, the novel enthralled me once again. I had read a lot in the intervening years, but I had never read anything like this book.

I did realize that *Hungry Hill* has antecedents, the most famous, and classical, of which is Thomas Mann's *Buddenbrooks: The Decline of a Family*. In *Buddenbrooks*, too, the family home and firm are lost as generations of men become progressively self-scrutinizing and, in business terms, degenerate. *Hungry Hill* is not du Maurier's only piracy of Thomas Mann: in her late novella *Ganymede*, a stuffy teacher of classics travels to Venice and is captured by a sinister homosexual underworld in a clear echo of *Death in Venice*.

Daphne du Maurier was in her way like Thomas Mann. Both were uncommonly respectable, deeply identified with and honored by their native countries, impeccably married, and clandestinely homosexual. In her literary persona if not in her actual novels, du Maurier stayed decorously within feminine boundaries; she never associated herself with literary giants like Mann. Instead, she compared *Hungry Hill* to

Gone with the Wind, an American, female-centered story of a single heroic generation that is entirely different from her own saga of failure and desiccation.

Like *Buddenbrooks*, *Hungry Hill* is a novel of degeneration and loss, but du Maurier's account of men slipping away from their inheritance has none of Mann's tragic dignity. *Buddenbrooks* begins with a generation of heroes or, at least, of capable men: the grandfathers, men of balance and tenacity who have seen the great Napoleon and who, like him, control their empire with ease and grace. In *Hungry Hill*, there are no heroes from whom the sons degenerate. Even rapacious Copper John, the founding Brodrick, loses his stature when, in his solitary old age, he marries his housekeeper. Mann might have called the declining descendants of *Buddenbrooks* men manqué;[4] du Maurier's are simply men. In *Hungry Hill* and her other male-centered novels, du Maurier provides no ideal of heroic masculinity from which the characters degenerate. Their doting passivity, their drunkenness and dependency, do not mark them as failed men but simply as men. It is this irreverent empathy with powerful males—not her supposed romantic sensibility—that makes Daphne du Maurier so consummate a woman writer.

According to Margaret Forster's superb biography, *Hungry Hill* had a special, wicked place in du Maurier's canon. Technically at least, its family was not her own: she appropriated the ancestors of the ever-willing Christopher Puxley, with whom she fell into intense flirtation while her husband was off being a hero in World War II. Puxley was less a lover than a harbinger of her leap beyond wifehood in 1947, when the self she called "the boy in the box" was released and she fell in love with Ellen Doubleday and then with Gertrude Lawrence. Her Irish saga of 1943 was an initial release of forbidden feelings, not all of them a lover's.

Usually she was lofty enough to ignore reviews, but those of *Hungry Hill* were particularly disappointing in their condescension. She saw her saga as a leap beyond romance, hoping—justifiably—that it would "set her in a different category as a novelist and silence forever dismissive references to *Rebecca* or *Frenchman's Creek*."[5] Throughout her life and beyond it, Daphne du Maurier was accepted only as a woman who could be dismissed. When I learned of the particular daring and disappointment that accompanied *Hungry Hill*, I felt a quiver of du Maurier's own genealogical occultism: I was born in 1943, the year of the novel's publication, and, reading *Hungry Hill* at the age of twelve as a forbidden treasure, I was rapt before I heard of *Rebecca*. My impassioned response to du Maurier's unappreciated venture into forbidden waters may not have been a mystic adoption of me on her part, but I do think she would have been heartened by my flashlight rituals.

Christopher Puxley generously shared his genealogy with the woman he loved, but his family was as unenthusiastic about *Hungry Hill* as the reviewers were. Christopher's mother particularly disliked its portrayal of the Puxley women, but the novel's pitiless account of male weakness may have been more mortifying, if less admissible. Moreover, since Copper John was modeled on Christopher's grandfather, Christopher inadvertently contributed himself to the devastating portraits of "Wild Johnnie," the lost alcoholic, and his lovably treacherous brother Henry, who gives up the estate, incarcerates his dynamic mother, and sells the mine.[6] Daphne played with the role of Christopher Puxley's lover, but as his chronicler, she was ruthless.

Rereading the novels that were so compelling when I was young, I am struck by their cruelty, even inhumanity. In *Hungry Hill*, the Brodricks are repeatedly brutalized, but their nemesis, the Donovan family, has no legitimacy, political or human. They are undifferentiated brutes, surging up from a subcivilized world. They exist to destroy all the institutions the Brodricks cultivate—the family, the estate, the mine—with no redeeming culture or kindness of their own.

Daphne du Maurier's politics are, baldly, appalling. In *Hungry Hill*, Anglo-Irish culture, however effete, is the only human alternative to the bestial populace. *The Scapegoat* is, politically, more horrible still. There is a subplot involving the Nazi occupation of France in which all the good peasant characters are collaborators; only Jean de Gué, profligate and heartless, fights for the Resistance. Jean's role in the Resistance is equated with his neglect of family, estate, and foundry, and finally with his ultimate sin: the assassination of Maurice Duval as a collaborator. Duval is the novel's lost hero; born a peasant, he is the ideal head of the foundry and, as the prospective husband of Jean's sister, of the family and estate. Jean's murder of Maurice is untouched by political commitment; it is an act of envy and perversity, a sin against the family.

I find Daphne du Maurier's lack of patriotic idealism somewhat titillating—at least when she deals with events like the French occupation that don't touch me directly (I do have to struggle with her anti-Semitism, anti-Americanism, and misogyny). The writer whose Resistance fighter is no hero, but a betrayer and a murderer, is the same diabolical child who disrupted the patriotic family dinner table at the start of World War I with the pseudo-innocent remark: "I like the Germans….I would like to have a German to tea with me here today."[7]

Moreover, there is something evilly feminine about her political allegiances: they are always a defense of home. The supposed collaborators in *The Scapegoat* are simply trying to keep the estate going; their allegiance is not to a nation but to daily life. In *The King's General*, her English Civil War novel, the central characters are so passionately Royalist that the Revolutionaries are treated as foreign invaders, with never an acknowledgment that they too are British. But Royalism in *The King's General* means the maintenance of a tenuous domestic existence in a Cornwall so self-enclosed that it is scarcely part of England. In both *The Scapegoat* and *The King's General*, domesticity is a vicious affair, riven with plots and jealousies, but grim as it is, it supplants national fealty.

Daphne du Maurier was a temperamental rebel, but she herself was no Resistance fighter. She was a collaborator throughout her life, not only with an England she saw as increasingly bleak and shrunken, but also with her own ancestral family. Hybrid, self-deluded, and soft, the du Maurier inheritance was the heart of her creative and created identity.

In *Hungry Hill*, the weakest, most betraying Henry gives the son he has dispossessed some futile advice: "It's a mistake … to walk back into the past. Look forward always, if you can" (p. 382). But her floundering Brodricks have nowhere to look but back, and neither does Daphne du Maurier's fiction, a continuing, aching tribute to a past that was never hers. In her unrevealing autobiography, *Myself When Young*, she writes without nostalgia about her privileged childhood, which she seems to have spent hating everybody, but she remembers tenderly a time beyond her life: "And why did a past that I had never known possess me so completely?… Always the past, just out of reach, waiting to be recaptured. Why did I feel so sad thinking of a past I had never known?" (p. 170).

That unknown past belonged to her father Gerald, the stylish and popular actor-manager. Beyond him, it belonged to his father, George, the first famous du Maurier. A popular *Punch* cartoonist, George du Maurier became a best-selling novelist at the age of fifty-six: his tender fantasies, *Peter Ibbetson* (1891), *Trilby* (1894), and *The Martian* (1897), made the French name famous and beloved throughout England. Fame and lovability, and an infectious melancholy, were George du Maurier's primary legacy to his son and granddaughter.

Gerald assured Daphne that his father was also an ideal family man: "Grandpapa—who died before Angela [her older sister] was born—with, D [Daddy, or Gerald] told us, a kind heart which made everybody love him, and a feeling for family that stretched to nephews, nieces, cousins and second cousins, so that any who needed help were not afraid to come to him, a man of very simple tastes unaffected by fame and fortune" (*Myself When Young*, p. 42). But, like so many writers of the 1890s, this domestic paragon was haunted by a lost world, the Paris of his youth. Daphne du Maurier coveted not so much her grandfather's fame or his kind heart as his memories of a vanished place.

It is odd, even perhaps occult, that I first encountered Daphne du Maurier and her grandfather in the same time and place. In the same summer camp where I escaped from conviviality into *Hungry Hill*, in the same summer of 1955, they showed old movies one night a week in a creepy old cabin called the Barracks. Then as now, going to movies was my favorite activity. On one memorable night, we saw John Barrymore in *Svengali*, an adaptation, though I didn't know it, of George du Maurier's *Trilby*. In the movie, Barrymore expands his great saucerlike eyes until their power stretches over the roofs of Paris, and Trilby's tuneless voice swells until she becomes a great diva. This sequence haunted me for years. Since I, like Trilby, cannot sing a true note, I was chilled and thrilled by the image of some great eyes reaching over the bunks of my camp until I would be metamorphosed into a brilliant singer.

I didn't know for years that *Svengali* had anything to do with any du Maurier. I did eventually, of course, see the Hitchcock movie of *Rebecca*, which is still, I suspect, as close as many people have come to du Maurier and her novel. The scene I most liked was an act of mesmerism similar to Svengali's: Judith Anderson as the evil housekeeper, Mrs. Danvers, tries to compel spacy Joan Fontaine, the nameless second wife, to throw herself out the window. The movie's domestic conflicts seemed tame, and I didn't care about Manderley, but this act of psychic possession turned a suspense movie into something larger.

Possessed in the same way by her father and grandfather, but repelled by them as well—as *Rebecca*'s second wife is by Mrs. Danvers, or Trilby by Svengali—Daphne du Maurier tried to capture memories not her own: memories of living in a lost, charmed country, of being a man, of being a tender killer of women. Since I am a scholar, I too am possessed by a past not my own: a Victorian England governed by well-meaning men and swarming with compliant women who, like Daphne du Maurier, had secret selves. When I learned that Daphne du Maurier's euphonious name encompassed a Victorian and a theatrical legacy she could neither share nor repudiate, I began to understand her fascination for me. I think I understand as well the power and privilege Daphne du Maurier gained by submerging herself in great ancestral men—and perhaps I also understand her loss of integrity.

2

The Men in Her Life

George Louis Palmella Busson du Maurier never forgot anything
he had lost: his noble medieval ancestors, his Paris, his artistic genius,
his left eye. His life, as he remembered it into myth, was a series of
bereavements. In 1851, when he was seventeen, he left his native
Paris for a London that seemed dead and dreary. In 1856, when he
was twenty-two, he returned to Paris as an art student, but his city
had been spoiled by Napoleon III's pompous renovations. He never
stopped missing the tangled, meandering, preelectrical, pre-Baron
Haussmann Paris of the bourgeois king, Louis-Philippe.

He might have been a great oil painter, he believed, but in 1857 he
suddenly went blind in one eye, a loss he described with ghastly precision: "I was drawing from a model, when suddenly the girl's head
seemed to me to dwindle to the size of a walnut. I clapped my hand
over my left eye. Had I been mistaken? I could see as well as ever. But
when in its turn I covered my right eye, I learned what had happened. My left eye had failed me; it might be altogether lost. It was so
sudden a blow that I was as thunderstruck."[1]

Living under the threat of a total blindness that never came, he settled into an easier life back in England. He married a motherly woman and consigned himself to the career of popular illustrator; eventually he became a still more popular *Punch* cartoonist. His best caricatures in the 1870s and 1880s ridicule precious aesthetic poseurs by placing them within the conventions of family life: games, dinner parties, china, all hopelessly prosaic by definition. George du Maurier's aesthetes are fools because they want to transfigure the homebound and commonplace, but in the role of winsome mythmaker, he himself would do just that. Later in his life, he wrote novels steeped in aesthetic longings, recording his losses and his dream of recovery of a time when life was art. Like a more sanguine Marcel Proust, George du Maurier wrote to recapture.

Though George du Maurier began a dynasty, he had no patriarchal ambitions. For his granddaughter Daphne, he loomed as a defining originary figure, the man who made the French name a British public endowment, but George himself longed only to regain his own origins among the nobility of medieval France. He was convinced that his grandfather, Robert-Mathurin Busson Du Maurier, was a gentleman glassblower who had been stripped of his estates and château by the French Revolution. A profound if self-effacing snob, he evoked his lost inheritance in dreamlike fiction. *The Scapegoat*, with its dilapidated château, bickering, deluded family, and crumbling glass foundry, is one of Daphne's mordant variations on her grandfather's pleasant dream.

That dream, in the form of *Peter Ibbetson*, became one of the few collectively consoling fables of the fear-ridden 1890s. *Peter Ibbetson* is a parable of miraculous restoration that centers on du Maurier's lost Paris. Like all of George du Maurier's work, the novel meanders through memories for over a hundred pages, whereas Daphne's fiction invariably begins with a terse shock. The first half of this long novel is a lingering account of a glowing past, softened in the memory of an exile and a prisoner.

Peter remembers bliss in an edenic Paris garden with his perfect, singing parents and bilingual games in a private language with a little girl named Mimsy. But his parents die and Peter is torn from his garden to a bleak London and the cruel guardianship of his villainous uncle, who is the grotesque descendant of a "Portuguese Jew, with a dash of colored blood in his veins besides."[2] Peter kills this monster and is put in a hospital for the criminally insane. There, his real life begins.

For Peter, as for many nineteenth-century men, growing up is a betrayal and an imprisonment. His sole longing, one that would haunt his descendants, is not to be free but to return:

> Oh, surely, surely, I cried to myself, we ought to find some means of possessing the past more fully and completely than we do. Life is not worth living for many of us if a want so desperate and yet so natural can never be satisfied. Memory is but a poor, rudimentary thing that we had better be without, if it can only lead us to the verge of consummation like this, and madden us with a desire it cannot slake. The touch of a vanished hand, the sound of a voice that is still, the tender grace of a day that is dead, should be ours forever, at our beck and call, by some exquisite and quite conceivable illusion of the senses.
>
> Alas! alas! I have hardly the hope of ever meeting my beloved ones again in another life. Oh, to meet their too dimly remembered forms in this, just as they once were, by some trick of my own brain! To see them with the eye, and hear them with the ear, and tread with them the old obliterated ways as in a waking dream! It would be well worth going mad to become such a self-conjurer as that. (pp. 193–94)

With the help of his Parisian playmate Mimsy, he becomes just such a self-conjurer. Mimsy, now Mary, Duchess of Towers—wise, grand, and, like all of du Maurier's favored women, exceptionally tall—returns and restores that past by teaching him the art of "dreaming true." Separated in body, they live together in glorious shared dreams that allow them to return to their childhood at will. Not only do they wander again with their families in the old, pre-Imperial Paris, they furnish their dream house with the masterpieces of Western culture.

Finally, they visit the deep ancestral past: having learned that they are relations, thus giving their love the soupçon of incest so enticing to du Mauriers, they join their common great-great-grandmother at her glasswork. Like the ingrown family in *The Scapegoat*, whose members are always on the verge of collapsing into each other, they merge with this venerable ancestor so that she can visit the future, and they, the past. For true dreamers, genealogy offers literal and personal immortality: "Ever thus may a little live spark of your own individual consciousness, when the full, quick flame of your actual life here below is extinguished, be handed down mildly incandescent to your remotest posterity. May it never quite go out—it need not!" (p. 361).

Dreaming with increasing skill, they regress back through French history to their primal ancestor, the first Mammoth. The dreams cease when Mary dies, but this goddess-like ambassador returns with consoling messages about the afterlife. Old and alone, Peter visits his still-young parents for the last time: "My mother is young enough now to be my daughter; it is as a daughter, a sweet, kind, lovely daughter, that I love her now—a happily-married daughter with a tall, handsome husband who yodels divinely and who has presented me with a grandson—beau comme le jour—for whatever Peter Ibbetson may have been in his time, there is no gainsaying the singular comeliness of little Gogo Pasquier [his own childhood nickname]" (pp. 413-14).

Ages, generations, even identities blur into a grand, embracing entity. Daphne du Maurier would find in this same family the same entanglement of ages, relationships, and roles, but hers was not generally a happy dream.

George du Maurier's amalgam of Spiritualism and science fiction, faith and despair, reads better than one would think: Peter's is so intimate a narrative voice, expounding with such plausible exactitude on the art of dreaming true, that only a curmudgeon would refuse to follow his modulation from memory into magic. Moreover, those of us who love nineteenth-century literature have lived with his boyish dreams. Eminent men from Wordsworth to Tennyson, from Dickens to Ruskin to Stevenson, wrote copiously about the longing, not only to relive their boyhoods, but to resurrect the vanished boy-self that lurked within manhood's masquerade: a longing that seems at best neurotic in twentieth-century America was articulated so often in nineteenth-century England that it came to feel universal.

Women were, and are, less avid to return to their childhoods; their forbidden yearning is generally to grow up. When she became her grandfather's biographer, Daphne du Maurier pitilessly exposed his fantasy of noble antecedents and a happy childhood. Nevertheless, *Peter Ibbetson* clings to her own private mythology. Her darkest, most disturbing books feature a visionary guide who teaches a yearning protagonist the art of "dreaming true," but the lesson is not as clear nor the consummation as beatific as her grandfather had wished.

Like all the du Mauriers, Daphne thought the tender, metaphysical *Peter Ibbetson* George's finest novel, but the sensationally popular *Trilby* hung over her career. Like all of George du Maurier's outsize women, the "very tall and fully-developed" Trilby is both angel and prophet.[3] Was she also, as an instrument of an old man's thwarted obsession, a prophecy?

Trilby deals less with family than with aesthetics. Robust and boyish, Trilby is the darling of the jolly art students studying and frolicking in Paris (as with the long beginning of *Peter Ibbetson*, du Maurier devotes the first half of the novel to romanticized accounts of his own youthful hijinks). British artists revere and paint her, but the Jewish musician Svengali invades her grand body for sinister ends: through mesmerism, he makes her the embodiment of his own aborted musical genius. As the acclaimed prima donna La Svengali, the seemingly superb Trilby is an empty puppet of twisted male artistry. When Svengali suddenly dies, she reverts onstage to her gauche, tuneless self, then pines lingeringly and dies enthralled, sighing "*Svengali…Svengali…Svengali*" (p. 340).

In *Trilby*, George du Maurier expressed his generation's hostile ambivalence toward the female artists who competed with them with unwomanly ambition. He himself had married a paragon of single-minded domesticity. Emma was, as her son-in-law put it, "an unfailing companion, always at hand and with no interests outside her home life. Placid in temperament, nothing ever seemed to move her strongly or excite her. She literally waited on her 'Kiki' hand and foot, each and every day, and lived only for him and her children." He hated feminists and female sensation novelists of the sort Daphne du Maurier would become in the twentieth century.[4] He would seem to have damned Daphne before her birth, but his Trilby is not a domesticated woman like his Emma. Rowdy and sexually experienced, she is more boyish than womanly—always, for the du Mauriers, a mark of distinction that preserved chosen select women from wifely obsequiousness.

Moreover, Trilby's voice may be tuneless, but her body is a work of magical art. In a famous speech, Svengali worships at the cavern of her mouth: "Himmel! the roof of your mouth is like the dome of the Panthéon; there is room in it for 'toutes les gloires de la France,' and a little to spare! The entrance to your throat is like the middle porch of St. Sulpice when the doors are open for the faithful on All Saints' Day" (pp. 55-57). And on his hymn goes.

In the same spirit, Little Billee, the English artist who sickens with love for her, reveres her enormous foot. Like Svengali, he immortalizes it—and himself—by painting it on a wall, a romantic consecration that so enthralled the novel's first readers that "trilby" became a synonym for "foot"; America elevated "trilby" to a chic brand of ladies' shoe. Trilby's foot was so important to the 1890s that it mutated into a series of such foot-shaped commodities as ice cream, scarf pins, and even a "Trilby Sausage." Trilby's voice is tuneless, but her body is an artistic and charismatic organ.

Trilby is a mixed inheritance for a granddaughter who would also become a novelist of the fantastic. In its many theatrical and film adaptations, Trilby herself is a vacuous victim of an evil male genius, but the novel is more eerily suggestive than its adaptations, as Daphne's own novels would be. Like du Maurier's grand Mary, duchess of Towers, the fictional Trilby is a benevolently demonic figure. She enervates the artists who love and invade her—Little Billee as well as Svengali—until they die pouring energy into her. This necromantic female presence would take over the composition of George du Maurier's last and maddest novel, *The Martian*.

Lovers of George du Maurier deplore *The Martian*, for it exposes the ravenous ego hidden within his persona's sweetness. *The Martian*, completed just before he died, is a heroic biography of himself—just the sort of biography his clear-seeing granddaughter didn't write. Its towering subject is the great writer and influential thinker Barty Josselin, a rampant self-glorification on du Maurier's part despite some coy narrative diversions.

Barty is a perfect physical specimen, loved by all, as brilliant (though untrained) in art, music, and literature as he is beloved. George du Maurier was generally self-deprecating about his work, but *The Martian* exposes the would-be genius concealed in the casual amateur: "His literary and artistic work never cost him the slightest effort. It amused him to draw and write more than did anything else in the world, and he always took great pains, and delighted in taking them; but himself he never took seriously for one moment—never realized what happiness he gave, and was quite unconscious of the true value of all he thought and wrought and taught!"[5] The influence of Barty's books, equaled only by Darwin's, extends throughout the world. Not only does his work prove the existence of an afterlife, but it also furthers human evolution: "And to whom but Barty Josselin do we owe it that our race is on an average already from four to six inches taller than it was thirty years ago, men and women alike; that strength and beauty are rapidly becoming the rule among us, and weakness and ugliness the exception?" (8: 853-54).

Suddenly, this advocate of strength and beauty loses his sight in one eye, as George du Maurier had. Blindness is a particularly humiliating male phobia in fiction of the 1890s. In a graphic process of degeneration, Rudyard Kipling's artist-hero in *The Light That Failed* goes blind in the middle of his story and wallows in unkempt self-pity; only a suicidal military exploit redeems him from total degradation. Barty Josselin is closer to classic blind male seers like Homer or Milton than he is to his maimed contemporaries. As he lingers on the verge of suicide, fearing he will go totally blind, Martia, his personified inspiration, descends to save him. Martia is a strapping woman from Mars who has always watched over Barty and those he loves, guiding and sometimes possessing them. She gives Barty medical and marital advice; she dictates more great works; she tells him how to save the race through selective breeding, beginning with his own magnificent descendants.

Martia is a strangely fallible goddess: she pressures Barty to marry a gigantic duchess, but he chooses instead a saintly Jewish woman named Leah—du Maurier's reparation, no doubt, for the anti-Semitism of *Peter Ibbetson* and *Trilby*. She then decides to come to earth as Barty's child, an embodied amalgam of sister, daughter, wife, lover, and mother who is an extreme version of the stew of family relationships du Maurier loved to concoct. But instead of growing into a duchess of Towers or a Trilby, little Marty falls out of a tree and dies; Barty and Leah die with her, George du Maurier himself died shortly thereafter; the human race remained untransfigured.

Marty fell out of a tree, but Daphne was born. Was Daphne the saving female descendant her grandfather had prophesied, sharing his consciousness and carrying him into the future? This novel that strains toward the future even contains among its characters an unrealized Daphne—Barty's energetic cousin, who bobs in for a few chapters and then disappears. Daphne du Maurier would later assume that she was named after a star of her father's generation, the irresistible Ethel *Daphne* Barrymore, who had the spirit to reject the infatuated Gerald; but her name is likely to have reached farther back, to an inchoate spark in her grandfather's prophetic soul.

As an unknown but pervading ancestor, George du Maurier must have been terrifyingly irresistible. Steeped in his mythology of generational transmission, *Peter Ibbetson*'s "little live spark of your own individual consciousness... handed down mildly incandescent to your remotest posterity," Daphne du Maurier experienced her legacy in an eerily intimate manner. She was not merely the granddaughter of a beloved writer; she was his little live spark.

Many of George du Maurier's less lovable attitudes remained alive within her. Like him, she was a snob, but unlike him, she never worshiped rank. Like him, she hated ugly little common people, especially if they were Jewish or American, but she never worshiped beauty.

She inherited his disdain without the progressive faith that fueled it. The perfectibility of the race is, in her work, a laughable idea: Daphne du Maurier's people are so avaricious and self-divided that they are beyond good and evil. George's passion for the past becomes equally forbidding in Daphne's fiction. George du Maurier's heroes weep for their lost boyhoods—the narrator of *The Martian* speaks for them all: "And I wake—and could almost weep to find how old I am!" (3: 50)—but Daphne du Maurier's characters could weep at any age, at any time, not at how old they are, but at what they are.

As an heir, Daphne du Maurier was bequeathed a bizarre private religion, a literary voice so lovable (at least on the surface) that it was impossible to emulate, and a vast audience encompassing theater- and, shortly, film-goers. She also inherited a towering image of herself as necromantic female descendant. All of George du Maurier's charmed tall women—Mary, duchess of Towers, Trilby, and Martia—are inspired seers, possessors of powers men can only yearn to touch. George du Maurier might have despised female sensation novelists, but his mythmaking art gave his granddaughter oracular stature.

In return, she wrote his life over and over; her entire fictional canon can be seen as an extended revised biography of George du Maurier. Though she poured on him none of the reverence Barty Josselin receives in *The Martian*, her acute family biographies display her cherished role as legatee. *Gerald: A Portrait* (1934), her family saga *The Du Mauriers* (1937), and "The Young George du Maurier"[6] depict with affection and wit the grandfather she never met, the origin of the du Maurier fame.

But she pitilessly uproots his tender family fantasies. The melancholy, ambivalent dreamer of *Peter Ibbetson*, torn between an idyllic France and a dreary England to which he is exiled by the deaths of his parents, was, in reality, a self-exiled failure: the family moved to England when George failed his *baccalauréat* examination, a disgrace that would have consigned him to a rank insufficiently elevated for his ambitious mother, who remained naggingly alive.

Daphne saw his undying boyishness less as idealism than as incapacity. Wavering, tender, an English paterfamilias suffocated by nostalgia for a romanticized France, he won love, as Daphne saw it, through his "irrational quality of tragedy": "There was something touching about his face, about his whole personality, that was impossible to explain. People longed to protect him for no reason."[7] Vicariously, she adopted his essential homelessness. The instability of the hybrid, this "half bourgeois, half Bohemian" wavering between worlds and identities, became her own legacy as well. She concludes *The Du Mauriers* with a veiled adoption of her exiled ancestor: "Kicky and Kicky's descendants hover in their characteristics between England and France, as do all hybrids who possess the blood of two countries in their veins" (p. 311). But her grandfather's French roots were not hers.

George du Maurier was sure, or claimed to be, that he was not just a displaced Parisian, but a dispossessed aristocrat. He told everyone, including himself, that his own grandfather, Robert-Mathurin Busson Du Maurier, a gentleman glassblower, had lost his estates and château during the French Revolution. But Daphne learned, and told, that Robert-Mathurin was an impostor.

Her superb research exposed Robert-Mathurin Busson: he was no dispossessed aristocrat but instead a revolutionary sympathizer who emigrated to England in 1789 to escape a charge of fraud. Robert had been a master, but never a gentleman, glassblower, much less a nobleman. On the way to England, he stole the name "du Maurier" from a local château; in England, he invented aristocratic ancestors whom his descendants proudly adopted. When he returned to France in 1802, he abandoned his wife and six children (one of whom was George du Maurier's father) in London. The magic name originated in betrayal and swindle.

Daphne revealed this hoax not only in her own family chronicles and her novel *The Glass-Blowers* (1963), a stilted account of her great-great-grandparents during the French Revolution, but also to George's official biographer, Leonée Ormond. Through Ormond, Daphne put discoveries that would have broken her grandfather's heart into the historical record. Ormond's *George Du Maurier* (1969) pays generous tribute to Daphne du Maurier (under her official title, Lady Browning—a title her grandfather would have relished), claiming that "this book could scarcely have been written without her help" (Ormond, pp. vi, 2)—especially in its account of the genealogical fraud on which George had based his private mythology. Ormond's biography is a debunking account of a compromised life that relies heavily on Daphne's acerbic revelation of ancestral delusions and deceptions.

She pillaged her grandfather's history, rejecting his faith but taking what she could use. George du Maurier beautified his parents; the shining center of *Peter Ibbetson* is the musical young couple in a French garden. *The Du Mauriers* (and Ormond following its lead) rewrites them as a wretched pair. George's father, Louis-Mathurin, was, in Daphne's view, a profligate betrayer, while Ellen, his much older mother, was hard and hating. In revision, they became a typical Daphne du Maurier couple.

Daphne annihilates George's ideal parents, but she recovers a lost hero: Ellen's mother, the courtesan Mary Anne Clarke. There is no Mary Anne Clarke in the family garden of *Peter Ibbetson*, but, as Daphne discovered, Mary Anne was the source of the family vitality and of its art. An English prostitute who ascended into an infamous Regency courtesan, Mary Anne was for a few years the lover of George III's brother, the duke of York. When the duke discarded her, she blackmailed him with old love letters; only his generous annuity prevented her from publishing her memoirs. This annuity supported the entire next generation. When Mary Anne's sour daughter married Robert-Mathurin's unstable son, they lived on this embarrassing inheritance until their own son George began to succeed. The suppressed story Daphne found, and wrote, was true source of *Peter Ibbetson*.

The Du Mauriers revises family myth to pay tribute to the unacknowledged family founder, an artful banished woman: "These fighting qualities were bequeathed to [George] by a woman, a woman without morals, without honour, without virtue, a woman who had known exactly what she wanted at fifteen years of age and, gutter born and gutter bred, treading on sensibility and courtesy with her exquisite feet, had achieved it laughing—her thumb to her nose" (p. 116).

Once again, Daphne exposed her grandfather's pretensions but found her own authorizing source, a woman the family was ashamed of, who had lived before the great men and subsidized them. She could not quite imagine the ancestor she found; her novel *Mary Anne* (1954) is as thin as *The Glass-Blowers*; but her research into her inheritance gave her a more urbane myth of origin than the charmed family her grandfather had believed in so ardently. As the historical embodiment of George du Maurier's giant, preternaturally potent women—perhaps as their hidden inspiration—Mary Anne Clarke freed Daphne du Maurier from paternal myths by giving her a myth of her own.

Daphne du Maurier's father was always, at heart, a son. Like Daphne, Gerald du Maurier lived in George's melancholy shadow even when he became "Sir Gerald" in 1922. His career took shape from his father's dreams: his first significant role was Dodor in a theatrical adaptation of *Trilby*. Since Dodor, a minor character, was based on George's feckless brother Eugène, Gerald began his stage life playing his own uncle as his father had re-created him. This familial immersion was a springboard to fame.

Neither Gerald nor his children had access to *Peter Ibbetson*'s yearning faith; George transmitted his discontented ache, not his visionary fulfillments. Epitome of the new, naturalistic school of actors, Gerald du Maurier was seductively relaxed on stage. He rejected the romantic heroism of the old Irving style, preferring instead, when he told an actress he loved her, to yawn, light a cigarette, and walk away. As Daphne described his oddly hostile anti-lovemaking: "He seldom kissed women on the stage, unless it was on the back of the neck or the top of the head, and then he would generally slap them on the face afterwards, and say, 'you old funny, with your ugly mug,' and walk away talking of something else as though he did not care."[8] The romantic transports of *Peter Ibbetson* had dissipated into a stylish animosity that would intensify in Daphne's lethal love stories.

Gerald specialized in gentleman-criminals: like their Victorian parents, Edwardian audiences loved actors in roles that emphasized doubleness and self-fabrication, and Gerald, for all his seeming ease, was the consummate double man. His signature roles were Raffles, his first gentleman-crook; Arsène Lupin, an aristocrat-crook; Hubert Ware, the insouciant and seemingly innocent hero of a courtroom melodrama, *The Ware Case*, who in the last act erupts into a different man, "hysterical, crazy, his nerve gone after the weeks of strain, screaming, in a horrible mixture of pride and remorse, that he was guilty all the time" (*Gerald*, p. 132); Barrie's Will Dearth in *Dear Brutus*, both in his failed self and, for an interval, as the tender father he might have been; and the role that still survives, Captain Hook/Mr. Darling in *Peter Pan*. Barrie did not write his pirate king and ineffectual father for the same actor: Gerald made it a double role. He could relax, it seemed, only when he was at least two people.

For Daphne, he achieved artistry only in the plays of Barrie, whose nostalgia for perpetual boyhood captured her father's heart. Gerald played fathers, but he lived *Peter Pan*, and the boyish Gerald was the man of his age. In 1910, he became manager of Wyndham's Theater. He was knighted in 1922, by which time he exuded the regal aura of the actor-managers who had dominated the theater since the 1880s. But Gerald was the last of a line extinguished by the commercialization—and, according to the clannish du Mauriers, the deplorable Americanization—of the English theater that followed World War I.

Daphne absorbed her grandfather's conservative nostalgia and her father's noblesse oblige, but she also inherited the family curse: a melancholy awareness that "it had all been too easy." The facility that enervated her grandfather was her father's bane and her own. *Gerald: A Portrait* shrewdly re-creates her grandfather writing *Peter Ibbetson*: "And now that he had started he found it simple, almost too easy; he wrote, in fact, with dangerous facility, as somebody once put it. The words poured from his pen" (p. 37). Within this gentlemanly ease lay the threat of artistic death.

But George's fantasies had been, for him, revelations; just as he had one blind and one seeing eye, he lived in two worlds, one mundane and one inspired. Gerald's double selves had nowhere to go. The coddled family baby who became famous with no apparent effort, Gerald, as Daphne depicts him, suffered from enervating depression and cynicism. His father's motto, "à quoi bon?" dimmed his energy. He fretted about the evanescence of performing; when he became a manager, he fretted about the ephemeral plays he put on; but he turned away from bolder projects that might jeopardize his secure position. *Gerald* refuses to sentimentalize his compromises and discontent. "He was constantly at war with himself and his own beliefs....Weakness and strength, shallowness and depth, nobility and poverty, intelligence and stupidity—all these qualities were his, and were at variance with each other, struggling for a supremacy none of them attained, making him a creature of great promise, baffling, lovable, but for ever unfulfilled" (pp. 105-6).

Gerald's sense of belatedness and incompleteness shadowed his fatherhood. He played a terrifying Captain Hook, "a tragic and rather ghastly creation who knew no peace, whose soul was in torment," as Daphne memorably described him (p. 82); but essentially he was Peter Pan, a perpetual spoiled son for whom aging was death. In a portrait steeped in empathy and condemnation, Daphne isolated the boy within the man: "He was inconsistent in all he did and all he thought. In many ways he was a child never come to maturity, shutting his eyes to the real treasures of life that lay within his grasp and living in a world of his own fantasy, bright yet tortuous with pretended pageantry" (p. 163).

Clinging to a paternal dream of boyhood that colored his onstage life, Gerald was scarcely a traditional father. Tormented by the sudden sexuality of his three daughters, who were barely younger than his many mistresses, he murmured to Daphne: "I wish I was your brother instead of your father; we'd have such fun" (p. 212). In a proposition too bizarre to appear in his biography, he went on to imagine dying, so that, like Martia in *The Martian*, he could return as his daughter's son (Forster, p. 53). In his own menacing fashion ("menacing" was the du Maurier code word for sexual attraction), Gerald acted the dream of *Peter Ibbetson*, in which parents and children, ancestors and descendants, lovers and brothers, become each other, dissolving in the family love-stew.

In a sense Daphne and Gerald had always been brothers, for the aging knight and the pretty girl were both boys at heart. In 1952, long after Gerald's death and the birth of her own children, her love affair with Gertrude Lawrence—who was, she wrote, "the last of Daddy's actress loves"[9]—reaffirmed their fraternity.

Daphne du Maurier's feelings for her father are hard to gauge, particularly since she expunges herself from his biography. She diagnosed herself with her generation's glib Freudianism: clearly, she was in love with him, thereby explaining not only her mother's dislike of her but also her own sexual attraction, at fourteen, to her flirtatious middle-aged cousin Geoffrey. *Gerald* coolly enumerates the great actresses who jilted her father before he married her compliant mother. One of them was the volatile Ethel Barrymore, whom the biography slyly calls by her middle name, Daphne, emphasizing not only the brilliance of the author's namesake but her forbidden sexual appeal. But since a Daphne also walks on in *The Martian*, it may be that both Gerald and his daughter were acting out fragments of George du Maurier's old dream.

Gerald was an enticing companion with whom Daphne identified, but he scarcely swept his cool daughter away. His importunate dependency frightened her; he was most menacing when he was a child, and he was fundamentally a child. At ten, she found his Will Dearth in J. M. Barrie's *Dear Brutus* (1917) more terrifying than his Captain Hook: she relished the poisoning pirate, but the loving father of a dream daughter sent her screaming out of the theater. The father-daughter scene in *Dear Brutus* is a midsummer illusion: the weak and profligate Dearth finds his imaginary daughter in a magic wood, but at the end of the scene he leaves her fading and crying, "Daddy, come back; I don't want to be a might-have-been." A murderous antifather was fun; a father whose love was potent enough to make her materialize and evaporate was a menace. Svengali and Will Dearth hovered around her, trying to create her or make her their might-have-been. The dedication of *Gerald*—"For Gerald and His Family," with no intimation that his family is also hers—describes her inheritance with cold precision.

She preserved herself not only by refuting her grandfather's mythology but also by creating her father. When, in 1932, Gerald died suddenly at sixty-one, she immediately began his biography; the astonishingly rounded and clear-eyed *Gerald: A Portrait* appeared the same year. As her father's biographer, Daphne has none of the rancorous indiscretion of a Christina Crawford or a Susan Cheever. She allows Gerald to exist in his own groping terms, just as she does the men in her novels. She herself enters the book only tangentially and in the third person, as a scowling or put-upon Daphne who pops in and out toward the end, just like the Daphne of *The Martian*.

The center of consciousness is Gerald himself, though occasionally she switches to the point of view of his doting mother, sisters, or wife. Expunging her own thoughts, feelings, traumas, and tributes, the twenty-seven-year-old novelist nestles in her father's mind and makes him experience his own story. The result is vividly dimensional, reminding us that the confessional memoirs in which twentieth-century Americans indiscriminately believe (especially when the confessor is a wounded woman) may be fun to wallow in, but often they see nothing and have nothing to tell. Unfeminine as it is, Daphne du Maurier's apparent emotional withdrawal facilitated an audaciously dramatic resurrection of a theatrical man.

The invisible daughter gives no quarter. Gerald's glamour and charm are there, but so are his mistresses, his instability, his terror of aging, his grasping emotional demands. Daphne is dry and devastating about her father's domestic scene stealing: "too much latitude [has been] allowed to these unconscious tyrants who move in a world of their own moods and whims" (p. 179). She re-creates frankly the strain of being part of a household of women that orbits around a spoiled father/child. Like Virginia Woolf's *To the Lighthouse* (1927), but with steelier self-effacement, *Gerald: A Portrait* exposes the tensions and inequities within an ideal Edwardian family headed by a childish great man.

In the du Maurier family, as in many others, men played inspired, self-creating boys while women fussed over them. Daphne's gracious mother and grandmother were content to foster men's careers and fuss about their health without dreaming of becoming even a Trilby; they raised Daphne and her two sisters, with the help of servants, from a discreet, womanly distance. Their primary children were their men.

George du Maurier had married a perfect womanly woman, of whom Daphne wrote in *Gerald*: "Pem was like a hen clucking after her chicks, wrapping them up for fear of draughts and dosing everyone within sight, including Kicky [George], with cod-liver oil" (p. 3). Gerald married the same deferential type; her mother, from whom Daphne felt unarticulated hostility, seemingly lived to worry about Gerald's "horrid colds." As the spectral Rebecca, this caretaking figure hovers in her perfection like a succubus over the nameless clumsy narrator. Women existed, it seemed, to dismiss children and fuss over childish men. Raised among exemplary ministering presences more dampening even than Trilby, Daphne became allergic to any role that required nurturing. The womanliness she saw refined her cold heart and keen eye.

J. M. Barrie's Wendy makes the exhausting journey to the Never Land only to be cast as the Lost Boys' mother. Although she is as buoyant as the boys, there is no other role for her, and there was none for bright flying Edwardian daughters—unless they wanted to play Peter himself. For Daphne du Maurier, it was easy to play Peter because Peter Pan was her cousin.

Like the multiple Gerald du Maurier, Peter Pan was not a single boy but a composite creature, inspired by the five sons of Arthur Llewelyn Davies and his wife, Sylvia, who was Gerald's sister. When, in 1928, twenty-four years after the first production, Barrie finally published one version of his ever-mutating play, he dedicated it "To the Five." By 1928, Arthur and Sylvia Llewelyn Davies were dead, and so were two of Barrie's cherished boys, but Peter Pan, like his namesake Peter Ibbetson,[10] played in his person a continually repeating past where there was neither death nor growth.

The three du Maurier girls called Barrie "Uncle Jim" just as their cousins the Llewelyn Davies boys did. *Peter Pan*'s Wendy Moira Angela Darling was partly named after Daphne's older sister, Angela du Maurier. Barrie was an intimate member of Gerald's family and a tender fabricator of Gerald, who starred in four Barrie plays besides *Peter Pan*. In fact, after exhausting himself pursuing such formidable artists as Ethel Barrymore and Stella Campbell, Gerald met his wife, an easier woman, when they were playing the young lovers in Barrie's *Admirable Crichton*. Barrie, it seemed, wrote the entire du Maurier family—or perhaps they summoned him to tell their story.

Peter Pan, whose subtitle is The Boy Who Would Not Grow Up, was the talisman of the du Mauriers. A du Maurier had given Peter his name; a du Maurier was mother of the original five; a du Maurier was their stage father and pirate nemesis. The du Mauriers were simultaneously Peter's parents and his boyish essence.

With this boy-worshiping inheritance, it was inevitable that Daphne du Maurier should play Peter Pan, and she did throughout her life, though she never played him well. As a child, she re-invented herself as Eric Avon, though Eric was a Rugby boy who excelled at games, not an elusive lord of shadows. As an adult, she persistently wore trousers, a provocative costume in the 1930s and 1940s, one easier to adopt once she sequestered herself in Cornwall. She came to pretend that she didn't know how to buy dresses.

Eager to please the remote mother who ostentatiously favored her son, Daphne's daughter Flavia made strenuous efforts to play her mother playing Peter: "Bing [Mother] despised girlish ways and, as I was no longer under Nanny's influence, I strived to please my mother in the way I dressed. I was dressed in cord trousers and boys' shirts, my hair cut straight and bobbed. . . . I developed into a tomboy, climbing trees and exploring deep into the Mena woods." Flavia's performance of Peter Pan was obediently suicidal: "I nearly hanged myself trying to fly like Peter Pan. I leapt from a high branch in a tree with a rope fastened about my waist. Unfortunately, the rope had slipped under my neck and I was rescued just in time by Mr. Burt."[11] Peter the apparent liberator was, like Trilby, a strangling ancestor for du Maurier women.

Daphne du Maurier was no towering Trilby, but neither did she look like a boy: blonde, blue-eyed, petite, she was a model of feminine English beauty. Flavia's memoir lets slip the fact that despite her mother's apparent indifference to her appearance, a beautician came every day to give her a facial (p. 199). Like being a proper woman, playing Peter Pan was work.

But of course Peter Pan looked no more like a boy than Daphne du Maurier did: he was inevitably played by a woman. That archetypal boy was never a boy, but a theatrical trouser role. His stage incarnation as a woman (never a child actress) suggests that Boy, that entity that lured three generations of du Mauriers and their scribe, is an alluring, unattainable condition for women and men alike.

In her novels, Daphne threw herself into shadow men, but these tormented, violent, self-divided creatures were never boys. Like Peter Pan, and like her grandfather and father, she yearned toward boyhood. Like the thwarted men who hovered around her, Daphne du Maurier never became a boy, but like them, she did, in her only authentic loves, conjure boys.

The Boy in the Box

Everything in Daphne du Maurier's world fed the glamour of boys. George and Gerald clung to boyishness, leaving adulthood to the ancillary women who took care of them. Those twin hovering Peters, her grandfather's Ibbetson and Barrie's Pan, presided over the masculine, nostalgia-drenched cultural establishment that the du Maurier family ruled and defined. Gerald doted on his daughters but gently pitied their femaleness. Accordingly, as a young mother, Daphne endured two daughters until she produced a boy, Kit, whom she smothered with love. Her male characters are her most distinctive achievement, but they are also her most unsavory. All her leading men are, in her words, "undeveloped, inadequate....Each of my five male narrators depended, for reassurance, on a male friend older than himself." Her three female narrators, on the other hand, "depended on no one but themselves" (*Myself When Young*, p. 66).

In Daphne du Maurier's novels and her life, men are paramount but defective and dependent. Unlike self-sufficient adults—who are women by definition—men are fully alive because they are boys at heart, as she was. She never abandoned her own boy-self, whom she called "the boy in the box,"[12] imagining that he, not Daphne, fell in love with women.

Incredibly, she not only adopted this talismanic boy for forbidden liaisons: she married him as well. Her husband was a dashing military hero who was also Boy—Major Frederick Arthur Montague Browning, called "Tommy" by his family and "Boy" by his regiment. After a few lively but uncompelling love affairs, a husband named "Boy" who sported all the paraphernalia of successful military manhood seemed to fill all the required roles. She married "Boy" Browning when she was twenty-five.

Like a Victorian novel, her autobiography ends with her simultaneous marriage and death. Introducing her future husband as "Boy" before listing his many other names, she quotes an entry from her diary assuring herself that having married Boy, she can kill the name that is her legacy: "I want to remember that I am doing this with my eyes open, and because I want a fuller life, greater knowledge, and understanding. So adieu…Daphne du Maurier" (p. 196).

She never married Boy in the essential way that George had married Peter Ibbetson, or Gerald, Peter Pan; she remained Daphne du Maurier and made the surname as famous as they had. She may never have achieved that fuller life, for in the 1970s, she told Martyn Shallcross, "My childhood in London and Cornwall I think was interesting, but I feel I was boring after my marriage."[13] Marriage made her neither mature nor boring, but it did, to a degree she never anticipated, force her to become the fussing, motherly woman she had always hated, for the boy in her manly husband was not the adventurous spirit of J. M. Barrie's dream.

Like many men of his generation, Major Browning was an unexpected combination of imperial fortitude and nervous delicacy. The man she first saw looked like a romance hero. As Margaret Forster describes him: "He was tall—six foot—with dark hair and grey eyes, very alert and energetic, and with a confident but not arrogant bearing" (p. 87). He was awarded the Distinguished Service Order in 1917 for his bravery in World War I, despite the fact that in 1916 he had been invalided home for eight months with the evasive diagnosis, "nervous exhaustion." He relived the war in shattering nightmares. These flashbacks were common among veterans—even Lord Peter Wimsey, Dorothy L. Sayers's omnipotent detective hero, ends his series weeping in his wife's enfolding arms—but Daphne du Maurier had not thought she was marrying a man she would have to take care of. She wanted men to enlarge her life, not to enfold themselves in it.

Tommy—or Boy, or, as she began to call him as he got glummer and glummer, "Moper"—had always had incapacitating stomach pains. These and other nervous ailments intensified as he aged. According to his daughter, he refused to travel without the toy bears he had had since childhood, whom he fondly called "the Boys." Since the British establishment likes boys, his career as a public servant remained exemplary. He was knighted in 1946 for his service as brigade commander in World War II; he was comptroller and treasurer to the royal family until he retired in 1959 under a strain no one he worked with perceived.

He was crumbling under illness and alcoholism. In 1957, he had a breakdown, and du Maurier was shocked to learn of his mistress in London: despite her own affairs with men and women, and despite the publication of *The Scapegoat* in the same year, she had never thought her Moper was capable of a double life. When he died, in 1965, she seemed scarcely to miss a marriage in which she had never been comfortable. She lived on in Cornwall until her own death in 1989. Having lost her literary voices, she died in despair, fading into a celebrated symbol of the landscape she had helped make famous.

She had never hated Moper, but she did hate being a wife. She loathed playing Mrs. Major Browning and listening to the other army wives, who seemed to her drearily oppressed. In 1937, during a miserable time when Tommy was stationed in Egypt and, as the major's wife, she was supposed to preside graciously over the regiment, she began *Rebecca*. *Rebecca*'s opening pages, where the drained couple live a suppressed existence in sunny, seedy exile, owe their intensity to du Maurier's own exile from damp, craggy Cornwall. The excruciating malaise of wifeliness at the British heart of the novel owes its intensity to du Maurier's exile from her former resilient self—or, as she would have put it, her boy-self.

Marriage to a war hero rather than an artist had promised to preserve her from her mother's caretaking role, but it didn't: Tommy's hidden invalidism exposed this confident model of a man as an actor like her father, and a boy like him too. Tommy "Boy" Browning turned out to have the boy's incapacity without his ability to take flight. Unlike her mother, though, Daphne was the breadwinner, the star, and the detached partner; she was still Daphne du Maurier, despite her obituary to the name. Marriage seems to have left her self-communion undisturbed. Her grandfather and father are stronger presences in her fiction than her husband is, though Boy does surface in one of her more bizarre tales.

"The Old Man" (1952) features a devoted old couple who live by the sea. There is something ineffably sinister about this loving pair. Gradually, we learn of their three daughters and a great hulking son named "Boy." Despite his majestic size and untapped strength, the narrator realizes that "Boy was just a great baby, and I have an idea he was simple."[14] He doesn't understand that he interrupts his parents' devotion. When he persists in hulking around, hanging on to his compliant mother and distracting her, his father murders him. "They were free to be together again, and there was no longer a third to divide them." Suddenly the story turns lyrical. In fairy-tale fashion, Boy's death transfigures his parents into swans. Emblems of beauty and freedom, they beat their powerful wings and "fly out to sea right into the face of the setting sun" (p. 230).

The beauty and power of birds are dangerous in these tales of the 1950s: "The Birds," an apocalyptic fable in which the birds of the world mobilize mysteriously against humans, appeared in the same collection as "The Old Man." "The Old Man," however, deals with domestic, not global, attack. Like a later tale, "The Chamois" (1959), in which a couple similarly solidifies their marriage by slaughtering a primitive and devoted creature, "The Old Man" exposes the murder on which marriage thrives. Loving couples devour outsiders.

But who, in Daphne du Maurier's secretive life, is the murdered Boy? Shadowy and suffering, he might be a response to Wendy's resonant greeting to Peter Pan: "Boy, why are you crying?" His robust appearance and fundamental helplessness suggest Boy Browning, the war hero who, like Boy in the story, "was no fighter. He didn't know how" (p. 228).[15] If "The Old Man" is Daphne du Maurier's *Peter Ibbetson*-like dream of her own erotic life, as its strange isolation from any generic context suggests, it may be a dream version of Boy Browning hovering around an exotic union whose exclusive intensity he is too needy to recognize, a union conceived by another Boy, the one du Maurier called "the boy in the box."

In 1951, when Daphne du Maurier was writing these tales, her own inner boy had sprung back. In 1947, she had fallen in love with Ellen Doubleday, wife of her American publisher, to whom she wrote passionately self-declaring letters. Always, she insisted, she wasn't "that unattractive word that begins with 'L'"; she was simply "a boy of eighteen all over again."[16] Her love of women was a separate thing from the lesbianism her culture whispered about with fear and loathing; it was a form of theater, a release of a suppressed self.

This pyrotechnical imagination of sexuality appears to go against the grain of lesbian literature. In the first half of the twentieth century, the clinical definition of lesbianism was as man-centered as Daphne du Maurier's view of the world: a lesbian was a man hidden in a woman's body, a man as imperious and authentic as du Maurier's boy in the box. Radclyffe Hall's lachrymose novel *The Well of Loneliness* popularized this view of the "invert"; after the novel was banned, attacked, and defended in a sensational trial, it became authoritative. In 1928, when *The Well of Loneliness* was published, suppressed, and fought over in court, Daphne du Maurier was twenty-one. If she bought the novel in Paris, as she was likely to have done, she learned little from its self-pitying rhetoric. Like *Peter Pan*, though, it would have taught her something about playing a boy.

Hall's Stephen Gordon has no alternative selves. She is destined to be an invert even by the parents who deplore her inversion: longing for a son and heir, they give her a boy's name. Everything brands Stephen: her name, her affinity with her father, her body, proclaim what she is.

> [She was uncommonly tall], handsome in a flat, broad-shoul-dered and slim flanked fashion; and her movements were pur-poseful, having fine poise, she moved with the easy assurance of the athlete. Her hands, although large for a woman, were slen-der and meticulously tended; she was proud of her hands. In face she had changed very little since childhood, still having Sir Philip's wide, tolerant expression. What change there was only tended to strengthen the extraordinary likeness between father and daughter, for now that the bones of her face showed more clearly, as the childish fullness had gradually diminished, the formation of the resolute jaw was Sir Philip's. His too the strong chin with its shade of a cleft; the well modeled, sensitive lips were his also. A fine face, very pleasing, yet with something about it that went ill with the hats on which Anna insisted...[17]

Stephen Gordon is an icon of integrity: from her name to her bones to her chin, she is male. Radclyffe Hall created a lesbian hero who knows no theatricality or deceit: to be a lesbian is to be Stephen is to be honest.

But this staunch figure is a theatrical creation. Like most women, Radclyffe Hall herself had no masculine inheritance. Stephen Gordon adores the honorable father she resembles, but her creator lived with-out a noble male reflection. Far from sharing with his daughter the "extraordinary likeness" of a resolute manliness, Radclyffe Hall's lazy father deserted the family shortly after she was born. Like most women, Hall was given no boy's name; like many lesbians of her generation, she chose one, "John." Implacable as it makes Stephen's destiny, *The Well of Loneliness* is no paean to self-realization; it is instead a dream of adopt-ing a male identity, a dream Daphne du Maurier shared.

The Well seems painfully literal in its equation of name, body, and sexual identity, but it keeps company with those other dreamlike works in which Daphne du Maurier was submerged. When Stephen Gordon and her lover Mary exile themselves in Paris, they read edifying books together, but the only one named is "that immortal classic of their own Paris, *Peter Ibbetson*," which inspires Mary to muse: "Stephen, if we were ever parted, do you think that you and I could dream true?" (p. 331). George du Maurier would never have dreamed of Stephen and Mary, but these forbidden women of the future dreamed his nostalgia into their inheritance.

It may not have been George du Maurier's Paris alone that lured Stephen and Mary, but his hovering, hybrid literary identity. Oscillating between worlds—Paris and London, art and domesticity, present and past, reality and dream—the author of *Peter Ibbetson* is as much a spiritual exile as Radclyffe Hall's half-women. Moreover, especially in *Trilby*, du Maurier pours his excruciating nostalgia into an ideal male community of frolicking artists that is lost forever when Trilby captures their love. Only a generation separates George du Maurier's charmed artistic clan from Radclyffe Hall's suffering, saintly community of female men.

Daphne inherited George's self-definition as a hovering hybrid, using his language to bridge a sexual chasm. During her futile, frenzied epistolary courtship of Ellen Doubleday, she wrote of herself, in a metaphor Stephen Gordon would recognize, as "a half-breed, …neither girl nor boy but disembodied spirit."[18] Ensconced in domesticity like her grandfather, she dreamed like him of impossible meetings in lost countries.

1928 was not only the year of *The Well of Loneliness* but also the year in which the play *Peter Pan* finally appeared in print. *Peter Pan* turns Radclyffe Hall's earnest inversions into a pageant. Stephen's love affair with caretaking Mary has affinities with Peter's mock-marriage to Wendy: like Peter, Stephen brings Mary into Never Land to make her a generic mother who keeps Stephen's house, sews on her buttons, chooses her clothes, and, when she works too hard, frets about her health. Single-souled Stephen never conceives of herself as an actor-manager, but, like the actress playing Peter Pan, she turns herself into a boy by staging her world and casting her intimates in supporting roles.

The Well of Loneliness looks like a manifesto of sincerity, but it is closer than it wants to be to the transforming theatricality of the du Mauriers. Like the du Mauriers and their presiding genius J. M. Barrie, Radclyffe Hall imagined multiple selves. She dedicates *The Well of Loneliness* suggestively to "Our Three Selves." Technically, this is a Spiritualist invocation: the "three selves" were Radclyffe Hall, her lover Una Troubridge, and her former lover "Ladye," dead by the time *The Well* was written but believed in, like *Peter Pan*'s Tinker Bell, and kept in the household through regular séances.

But "our three selves" could have a less specific meaning, one evocative of a charmed spectral Boy, the Stephen Gordon who, unlike actual women or men, is a pure male.[19] In the same spirit, Barrie's dedication of *Peter Pan* "To the Five" refers literally to the Llewelyn Davies boys but conjures also the many entities needed to compose a Boy who could never exist. Both the Never Land of *Peter Pan* and the underworld of *The Well of Loneliness* are haunted by a boy who is not a boy, the same entity who blessed Daphne du Maurier's secret selves.

If Daphne du Maurier did know *The Well of Loneliness*, she imbibed not its sincerity and suffering but its transformations. In the first half of the twentieth century, lesbianism was associated with dual personalities: popularized largely by the notoriety of *The Well of Loneliness*, a shadowy male transmitted his instincts to women who loved women, endowing that love with theatrical as well as Spiritualist potential.[20] Lesbianism was alluring because it was neither natural nor female.

Daphne du Maurier had no affinity with femaleness or with nature unless it was Cornish. When she fell in love with Ellen Doubleday, the boy who came bursting out of her box was not only her long-suppressed eroticism but also a revelation of alternative selves akin to *Peter Ibbetson*'s. The roles in which she cast herself in her letters to Ellen have much in common with Stephen and her Mary, and also with Peter and his Wendy: she vowed to become, in Ellen's time of trouble, "'a kind of clear-thinking brother, who holds your hand.' But at the same time Ellen was to remember, 'You are the mother I always wanted'" (Forster, p. 238).

There was no possibility that Ellen Doubleday would respond: she was as traditional a womanly woman as the du Maurier wives. In a characteristically theatrical transference, the actress Gertrude Lawrence inherited Ellen's role by playing Stella Martyn—who was modeled, du Maurier claimed, on Ellen the perfect woman—in du Maurier's play *September Tide*.

Gertrude Lawrence played an exemplary feminine woman in *September Tide*, but offstage, her role generated a less conventional love story than anybody wrote for her. "The last of Daddy's actress loves" and "the boy in the box" were lovers until the actress' sudden—and, for Daphne du Maurier, devastating—death in 1952. When she died, Gertrude Lawrence was playing the wise, maternal Anna in Rodgers and Hammerstein's beloved musical *The King and I*. Anna goes to Siam as a civilizing angel, and she does, in the course of the play, correct its gorgeous barbarism. As in *September Tide*, whose Stella is a paragon of old-fashioned, "positively World War One" womanhood in contrast to her strident, sloppy postwar daughter, Gertrude Lawrence is enshrined in *The King and I* as a Victorian angel of gentle governance—as another stage Wendy playing mother in Never Land.

But, like Wendy, Anna has an underside articulated in Lisa Ben's underground parody of her song "Hello Young Lovers." In Rodgers and Hammerstein's original song, widowed Anna reassures a series of pitying couples, "I've had a love like you." This anthem to marriage became, in the underworld of the 1950s, "All you cute butches lined up at the bar, / I've had a love like you."[21] Like Daphne du Maurier, Gertrude Lawrence played her role so well because she was also something else. The shadow boy adds piquancy to the good woman, just as, in dream plays like *The Well of Loneliness* and *Peter Pan*, the woman's body lends intensity to the boy she is.

The explosive and unexpected liaison between Gertrude Lawrence and Daphne du Maurier brings us back to the sacrifice in "The Old Man," which was written during their love affair. If its Boy is Daphne's suppressed and now importunate inner boy—cousin of Stephen Gordon, Peter Pan, Peter Ibbetson—his murder might portend the death of a theatrical idyll. In this reading, Boy is killed by the snuggly insularity, and the innate viciousness, of heterosexual coupledom. Daphne can go back to one Boy only by killing the other.

But if Boy is Boy Browning, this story of transfiguration becomes a covert lesbian allegory in which, after murdering the needy husband/son, the devoted women metamorphose into soaring swans. Radclyffe Hall and the specialists from whom she learned about herself tried to believe that she and all women like her were males in their essence. Daphne du Maurier embraced the play within their declaration of integrity. She imagined no single essence, but a glorious activity, transformation into a creature beyond humanity, a creature who, in "The Birds," is potent enough to destroy the fragile human race. She told Ellen that her male incarnation was, like Peter Pan, genderless, "neither girl nor boy but disembodied spirit." If "The Old Man" is a guarded account of her own romantic triangle in 1951, it imagines no resolution, but only unending murder and metamorphosis.

Daphne du Maurier would never write novels as cryptic and many-sided as her tales; perhaps in deference to the men in her life, her novels are clearly plotted, straightforward (though never simple) narratives in which we never doubt what we see. Only in short tales like "The Old Man" did she plumb a prismatic and sinister world where identities mutate and murder has no narrative rationale. Her best tales reflect her melange of lives and her multiplicity of roles, for the boy in the box was not the only, or even the hidden, Daphne du Maurier. This woman who studied men, who felt with them, who emulated and played them with uncanny authenticity, also assumed a quintessentially female role: that of family chronicler.

3

Family Chronicler

As I was writing the chapter you've just read, I realized that I too am a family chronicler, though the families I study are never my own. The du Mauriers were an expansive clan, embracing changes in art and culture; their expressiveness allows me to visit a family without being trapped in it. When I discovered *Peter Ibbetson* lurking within Daphne du Maurier's darker self-divisions—and even within *The Well of Loneliness*, a novel George du Maurier would never have read and whose very existence would have pained him—the same thrill came over me as when I was writing the final chapters of my last family saga, *Ellen Terry, Player in Her Time*.[1]

Like this one, *Ellen Terry* is a theater book, and a book about an actress transforming herself into a womanly woman, winning love, and losing her best parts. The Victorian actress Ellen Terry wooed decades of audiences. Like Daphne du Maurier, she was a blonde, feminine, quintessentially English rose. Tirelessly, she adapted her femininity to changing times and tastes, suppressing, to her psychic cost, all forbidden roles and inadmissible selves. But those lost selves lived on in her two abrasive modernist children who shunned her compromised West End triumphs.

To me at least, those children, Edith and Gordon Craig, were the stars of *Ellen Terry*, for although their roles were comparatively small, and although the theaters they shaped were experimental, obscure, even antitheatrical, their rebellious art perpetuated their mother's denied identities. The transplantation of the Victorian Ellen Terry, and all she represented, into an edgy, fractured twentieth-century theater that tried to renounce her was, as I saw it, the great achievement of my family saga. Ellen Terry's refractory children staged for their mother a drama of transformation and survival—the survival not only of a woman but also of the cultural worlds she incarnated. As a personification of Victorian expansiveness, Ellen Terry lived on in shadowy form—and lives still—in the sparer, smaller, more fearful culture of the twentieth century.

For at least a generation, *Peter Ibbetson* underwent the same mutation in the crucible of new women and new worlds, worlds that denied everything George du Maurier thought he stood for. As *Peter Ibbetson* twists through Daphne's more sinister fictions, we see in the fraught relationship between self-divided ancestors and nervous heirs cultures dying and preserving themselves, faiths evolving, artistic assumptions re-forming.

I can't imagine myself playing any role in the Terry/Craig or du Maurier dynasties. My relation to these glamorous households is something like that of a Victorian governess sitting silently in a corner, watching patterns form and decompose. I can see how they work, what they do to and for each other, but I am not of them. I am not blonde or rosy or Anglo-Saxon; I could never cope with ancestors who perpetuate themselves down the generations. Both Ellen Terry and George du Maurier were, like all Victorian artists, great mythmakers. Their children, like their audiences, lived their dreams even when they thought they were free.

These Victorian ancestors were so invincible, despite their self-effacing manner, that they were remarkably indulgent with their children—far more than my own enlightened American parents were.

I suspect that Ellen Terry and the du Mauriers gave their children such license because they knew those children could neither live nor create without them. When her daughter and son floundered, Ellen Terry insisted that her partner, the great Henry Irving, accommodate them in his exclusive Lyceum company; when they went off on their own, she graced their way. She subsidized Gordon Craig's flamboyantly uncommercial productions, supported his many illegitimate children, and made important theatrical contacts for him long after she knew his arrogance would cripple his career beyond repair.

Tirelessly, though, she went on making lives for her stubborn children. She organized a series of cosmopolitan venues for her withdrawn daughter, Edy. When these came to nothing, she arranged Edy's lesbian union and managed with flair her daughter's unorthodox household. Whether her children fled to her or from her, and both did both throughout their long lives even after she was dead, she arranged their existence, professional and domestic, with the artful fluidity of a great director.

Daphne du Maurier's life was similarly well arranged; Gerald pitied and exploited her femaleness, but he never tried to suppress her talent. The du Mauriers didn't consider sending the sophisticated young beauty to one of the new women's colleges that were struggling for recognition in the 1920s, but then she never wanted to go: she was too stylish and insouciant to lock herself up with grim pioneers. Her literary talent delighted the family: Gerald proclaimed that she had inherited George's spirit and proudly marshaled his formidable contacts on her behalf. In 1929, her first story was published with great fanfare in her Uncle Willie's fashionable magazine, *The Bystander*. *Myself When Young* claims airily that her family was equally eager to set her up as a movie star: her dilemma was which career to choose! In the middle of an international depression, when even the most determined young women had to struggle to be heard, her royal name and inherited facility made love and work dangerously easy to win.

Am I jealous of those chosen children of great mythmaking performers? Probably, but just as I can't imagine being a mythmaking ancestor, implanting faiths that would shape generations, so I can't imagine living as a descendant without resistance. My family life has been a series of discontinuities (never breaks) rather than a single story—or even, like Daphne du Maurier's, conflicting stories—handed down, rejected, remolded, and retold. Four generations ago, my great-grandparents came here from somewhere in eastern Europe, but no one, not even their children, knew exactly what countries they left. Some of my friends are having fun tracing their genealogies, but even if I could recover our name and nation, I wouldn't. I don't blame my great-grandparents for not transmitting our history: there are no châteaus in my family's mythic past. Our origin is untalked about and our Americanness is still tenuous after more than a century: the New York City we all cling to is not quite embedded in America or any nation.

Our family possessions were not collective myths but children, of whom I am one of the oldest. The older generation's mission was to keep us firmly in the nest; ours, as I see it, was to make lives on our own terms. Because we had no ongoing narrative, transmitted over generations, I can't imagine *not* having formed myself in opposition to what I was told to be—particularly since I was raised in the timorous American 1950s, in whose mandates of conformity and compliance it was impossible for any sensible woman to believe. Because I felt that I invented (or discovered?) my life, my adult self is myself alone. Nothing I do represents a collective vision. This solitary individualism is no doubt a traditionally American way of being and perceiving, but capacious English lineages remain enthralling to me, though no doubt even in England today there are few families as indulgent, yet as entwined, as the du Mauriers were.

Precious as they were, isolated as they thought themselves, the du Mauriers were never cloistered: even their most bizarre psychic twists seem larger, more representative, than the oddities of ordinary families. Like Ellen Terry, they were spectacular even when they felt alone. Even du Mauriers who weren't actor-managers like Gerald were radically theatrical: though George's *Peter Ibbetson* was undramatized until 1917 and inspired only one lackluster film, *Trilby* leaped beyond the page from its inception. In 1895, its first production, starring Herbert Beerbohm Tree as Svengali, was such a sensation that it made an easy transition to the screen. The most literal adaptation is John Barrymore's *Svengali* (1931), but a host of classic films about female performers and their magnetic mentors (*The Red Shoes, The Seventh Veil, Limelight, The 5,000 Fingers of Dr. T*, all three versions of *A Star Is Born*) owe their essence to *Trilby*. George du Maurier's material is so inherently spectacular that it radiates throughout film history.

In the same way, though Daphne's own two plays are relatively lifeless, she flourishes on film. Like her grandfather, she is perpetuated in performance. As with George, whose original *Trilby* is only intermittently in print, Daphne is known largely through film adaptations of her novels and stories, especially Alfred Hitchcock's *Rebecca* and *The Birds*; audiences who see the films over and over may never have read a word of her books. The essential theatricality of all the du Mauriers, even those who wrote little but fiction, makes their family saga symbolic just as great actors become symbolic merely by entering. The du Maurier family was not an enclave but an epitome. As they revised each other, they took the world with them.

Daphne's family chronicles have little in common with the genealogical craze so popular among rootless American intellectuals in the late twentieth century. Most Americans turn to genealogical research to locate, or imagine, a continuity we have never known. We make pilgrimages to Ellis Island; we imagine mystic kinship with some disembodied name we know only from archives or the Internet; we fabricate roots that would explain our inconsistencies, dislocations, false starts, endless endings.

Daphne du Maurier knew her ghosts, many of whom were also her grandfather's, before she knew herself. Her unflagging research into family chronicles—of other families as well as her own[2]—was not, like that of most Americans, an attempt to fill an emptiness, to turn discontinuities into transitions, nor was it an exorcism of a past that was crowding her out; she saw her ancestors as fragments of herself. Thus, her research was inseparable from her fiction and from her lifelong discovery of multiple selves.

Her enthusiasm for research, for which she gets no credit from those who see her only as a palpitating fantasist, is my great bond with Daphne du Maurier. I too search through the past, but, like that of most Americans, my research is rife with contradictions. Even as I write this book, I wonder what makes me disinter a woman so coldly exclusive, so dismissive of women, so eager to banish outsiders as "honks"—her code for "lower class"—so condescending about Jews. For Daphne du Maurier, to know the past was to know herself. For me to know Daphne du Maurier is, perhaps, to know, and to love, an enemy.

She claimed the past she studied, but she never inserted herself in it. Her du Maurier family chronicles, both nonfictional and novelized, are models of self-abnegation. Her best novels are steeped in the psyches of their narrators, but when she turns to her own family, narrators disappear. *Gerald* is startling in the brilliance of its portraiture and the absence of its "I"; in *The Du Mauriers*, which followed in 1937, Daphne—heir, storyteller, soon-to-be-famous novelist—withholds herself entirely from the narrative. *The Du Mauriers* tells the story of George's unhappy parents, a story that is at heart a tribute to her own great-great-grandmother Mary Anne Clarke, the expurgated woman behind the proud name:

> Funny that the fortune [George] would build up, and which would embrace so many of them, sprang from that first ten pounds his mother gave him—ten pounds from her annuity, the annuity that Mary Anne won with her determination and her wit. A stroke of the pen in 1809 decided the fate of so many little unborn men and women. A crude and rather sordid bargain between a prince and a prostitute started a cluster of threads that stretched their way across the world and set so many puppets dancing, some happily, some wearily, but all with an infinitesimal shrug of the shoulder and the ghost of a smile.[3]

Having discovered this disreputable puppet master, Daphne leaves her alone. Written just before *Rebecca,* during Daphne's wretched Egyptian exile as army wife and uneasy mother, *The Du Mauriers* might have been an outlet for the author's loneliness, frustration, and self-questioning dissatisfaction, but it is not. Nervously, restlessly, it probes heredity, but the inheritance is never hers:

> Was Gyggy [Eugène] a charming waster all his life because his grandmother had been a wanton? Was he a rebel because his mother had not wished him born? Was Kicky [George] a meticulous draughtsman in maturity because of Louis-Mathurin's scientific exactitude, and because Ellen had talent in her fingers? Did that longing to escape from his surroundings, that almost unbearable nostalgia for the past, exist in him because his father's father, Robert Mathurin Busson, had been denied his country and had lived in exile for over twenty years? What sort of legacy could this Robert Mathurin hand down to his children, all born to him in an alien land when he was over fifty, but a sense of yearning and frustration, a desire to return, an ache for things known and experienced in the subconscious and in the blood? (p. 115)

The author, herself an exile in an alien land who is about to begin a novel about an "almost unbearable nostalgia for the past," asks probing questions that leave her own life unexamined. How should we respond to this determined invisibility? In our own therapy-drenched age, family chroniclers spill their needs and obsessions all over their material: ancestors cannot exist without the emotions, questions, regrets they arouse in undreamed-of descendants.

If Daphne du Maurier were writing *The Du Mauriers* today, we wouldn't have to wait sixty years for her biography: we would hear all about her dislocation, her resentments, her irritation at her husband's nervous stomach, her ambivalence about her baby daughters. But we might learn little about the du Mauriers. As she was, she wrote about her husband only obliquely and allegorically, about her children, not at all, and about herself, never, until her late and chiseled memoirs,

Myself When Young, Vanishing Cornwall, and the six slight essays in *The Rebecca Notebook and Other Memories*. In these days of pseudo-intimate talk shows and pain-drenched memoirs, most readers will find it hard to forgive Daphne du Maurier for refusing to confess—especially considering her reputation as a woman's writer. Perhaps I stand alone in admiring the impersonal clarity and literary tact of her two family chronicles. It would be easy to psychoanalyze that impersonality or dismiss it with words like "repression" or "denial," but I find Daphne du Maurier enviable in her theatrical freedom to disappear. I too find it "a tell-him" (du Maurier code for "boring") to write about myself at length, though I'm writing about myself right now. Like Daphne du Maurier, I emerge, I think, in what I see; instead of confessing, I explore strange cultures like that of Victorian England, recognizing myself—sometimes—where I never was.

It might be impossible now to be as withheld as du Maurier was when writing about her ancestors, but for me she is an antidote to our own self-obsessive trauma mongering. Her great gift as a writer is her ability to write, often uncannily, about the many people she is not. She reclaimed and redefined her family, but she was not lost in that family. Often, she is sardonic about her characters; many of her people, relations or otherwise, are appalling or insane, but never does she drench them in her own sensibility. By letting her people alone, she displays not only an artist's discrimination but also an authentic researcher's respect for the past.

Her two fictional chronicles were written many years after *Gerald* and *The Du Mauriers*, as a respite, it seems, from turbulence. *The Glass-Blowers* (1963) goes back beyond *The Du Mauriers* to trace the story of the Busson family's self-serving evolution into the du Mauriers during the French Revolution. *Mary Anne* (1954) tells the complete story of the shrewd courtesan whom Daphne cast as the family's secret smiling divinity and her own ancestral inspiration. Does it make sense to say that I admire these two novels because they are both so dull?

The Glass-Blowers purports to be about the French Revolution, but it is no bodice-ripper; no one is guillotined; no blood runs in the Paris streets. Like the Irish Rebellion in *Hungry Hill* or the German occupation in *The Scapegoat*—or, most relentlessly, the birds in "The Birds"—great historical events exist only to smash the novel's chosen family and, in this novel, to threaten its collective creation, the glass foundry. Here as throughout du Maurier's fiction, history offers neither melodrama nor insight; it is random catastrophe.

The novel is dedicated "To my forebears, the master glass-blowers"; its animating symbol is a crystal tumbler made in the family foundry for the visit of King Louis XV. The story begins with an imagined encounter: dutiful matriarch Sophie Duval, the novel's chronicler and presiding domestic spirit, gives the tumbler to young George du Maurier with an inspiring blessing: "My father used to say that as long as it remained unbroken, treasured in the family, the creative talent of the Bussons would continue, in some form or other, through the succeeding generations."[4]

Of course, the real George never learned the truth about his family's French past, nor did he receive in compensation an engraved tumbler meant for a king. Daphne wrote *The Glass-Blowers* to destroy her grandfather's wistful dreams of aristocratic ancestors and lost châteaus, but, in the guise of Sophie Duval, she gave him a talisman she could respect.

The tumbler is not only a modest replacement for her grandfather's fantasy of origin; it is an equally modest rebuke to her own age as well. As a symbol of carefully wrought art carried over nations and generations, du Maurier's family glass might be a sardonic corrective to an American Glass family who, in 1963, was reaching its apogee of popularity.

J. D. Salinger's seven Glass siblings were, in the 1950s and early 1960s, the saints of American youth. They were the family we all wished we were beautiful and delicate enough to belong to. The seven Glasses had bohemian, affectionately irrelevant parents; with the exception of one tangential sister, they had no children. Sensitive, inbred, shattered by the suicide of their presiding elder brother, Seymour, in the beloved inaugural story, "A Perfect Day for Bananafish," they communed within themselves alone. Their mission, in the cluster of stories that traces their spiritual and artistic crises, is to avoid the lure of Seymour's death and to stay alive in an intolerable world.

Salinger's Glass family is everything the du Mauriers were not.[5] The du Mauriers were fraudulent aristocrats, but, in supposedly democratic America, the Glass family became authentic royalty to those of us who believed in them, for they were talented, brilliant, beautiful, and, above all, wounded in their souls. Their name is a token, not of achieved artistry, but of saintly fragility. In midcentury American culture, the mission of an aristocracy of Glass is to break.

The same is true of Laura Wingfield's glass unicorn in Tennessee Williams's play *The Glass Menagerie* (1944), another beloved account of sensitive souls too breakable for a coarse world. Families of Glass would become American national icons because they were too precious to endure: when they broke, they indicted all of us who coarsely survived. In the middle of the twentieth century, America ruled the Western world and had the ammunition to destroy the entire world, but its heroes were paragons of charmed incapacity.

Daphne du Maurier's glass-blowers have more stamina; they are precious because they do survive, valuable because, like their glass, they are carefully wrought but *not* fragile. Through swindling, through doggedness, through artistry, her glass-making family lives on—unlike the American Glasses—to compose a saga, that sprawling, spreading, biblical form so uncongenial to midcentury Americans, who were concerned only with the uniqueness of a single delicate generation.

In the Busson family that dominates *The Glass-Blowers,* no one is unique and there is no one to love. Its revolutionaries are obsessed losers; its survivors are turncoats or, like chronicler Sophie, drudges. Du Maurier's refusal to woo her reader's sympathy is her refusal to be an American heart-tugger, her refusal even to be Daphne du Maurier as that writer was popularly understood. In the collective littleness of the Busson family and the token they nevertheless pass on, the tricks of the novelist defer to the integrity of the chronicler.

Sophie, the surrogate for dutiful family chronicler Daphne, exists solely as a custodian, both of the lost family past in an era of dislocation and of the next generation. Meditating upon the "great gulf between our time and all that had gone before," she does her best to close that gulf by making herself the repository of that vanishing past. When her revolutionary sister Edmé pinions her with the accusation, "You are not a patriot," Sophie can only ruminate: "I understood nothing except that I was a woman near her time, carrying a baby that might be born dead even as Cathie's had been, and I had narrowly escaped death myself by being caught up in a screaming mob which had no knowledge why it screamed" (pp. 179-80). Motherhood and patriotism are irreconcilable.

In fiction by American women, from Margaret Mitchell's *Gone with the Wind* to Toni Morrison's *Beloved*, babies are the raw material of historical crises: giving birth implicates obscure women in the casualties of their times. Daphne du Maurier is less romantic about the importance of mothers in the great world. Patriot and parent share nothing; one flings herself into a dream of the future, the other preserves what she can of the past. Drawing firmer boundaries than Mitchell or Morrison, du Maurier produces a novel that is unabashedly dull. As the gatekeeper of the family—perhaps even the ancestor of heroic Maurice Duval, the martyred caretaker of occupied France in *The Scapegoat*—Sophie does little of interest. Unlike du Maurier's more estranged narrators, she does not even perceive in an interesting way. But her unimaginative inaction is, for Daphne du Maurier, the essence of the research in which lost worlds are stored.

Sophie Duval is neither patriot nor romantic, but her caretaking is the mission of du Maurier's female narrators, all of whom chronicle dying worlds and, for as long as they can, prop up the men who represent those worlds. Honor Harris, the narrator of *The King's General*, is forced into stasis: crippled in a riding accident when she was a daring young girl, the immobilized woman can do nothing but tell the bleak story of the failure of the Royalist cause during the English Civil War. The nameless, helpless narrator of *Rebecca* plays the same static part: paralyzed by dread of her imperious husband and Manderley's imperious traditions, she can only chronicle the doom of man and estate. For Daphne du Maurier, there is only one role available to a female storyteller: that of immobile chronicler, preserving the worlds men have lost.

Mary Anne has no dutiful, storytelling Sophie to act as foil to the daring heroine of the title. Du Maurier rarely wrote in the third person, but when she told the story of the woman she saw as her true progenitor, she wrote something rare in her canon: a thesis novel, and a feminist thesis novel at that. Unlike *The Glass-Blowers*, *Mary Anne* was written not to chronicle ancestral losses but to speak out.

Mary Anne was marketed to resemble Kathleen Winsor's racy bestseller, *Forever Amber* (1944), but *Mary Anne* is no spectacle of historical lubricity; its courtesan heroine is not so much sexy as smart. She loves words and books; in another age, she would be a novelist; but in Regency England, as her story illustrates, women who write are dangerous. Power lies in being a whore, a role she plays with gusto and good humor. Like Thackeray's Becky Sharp—the engaging creation of George du Maurier's favorite author—Mary Anne makes herself all things to all men, including, for a charmed time, the king's brother, the duke of York.

But unlike Becky Sharp, Mary Anne thinks, and tells us what she thinks. From her first foray into the alphabet, her conclusions are not flattering to rulers: "The *a*'s, the *e*'s, and the *u*'s were women; the hard *g*'s, the *b*'s, and the *q*'s were all men, and seemed to depend on the others."[6] As a young girl, she realizes that these helpless creatures are also, somehow, masterful, a paradox that generates a complaint rare in du Maurier's writing—rare, in fact, in any novel written by a woman in the 1950s:

> Then men were not dependent upon women after all, as she had thought—women were dependent upon men. Boys were frail, boys cried, boys were tender, boys were helpless. Mary Anne knew this, because she was the eldest girl amongst her three young brothers[.]…Men were also frail, men also cried, men also were tender, men also were helpless. Mary Anne knew this because her stepfather, Bob Farquhar, was all of these things in turn. Yet men went to work. Men made the money—or frittered it away, like her stepfather, so that there was never enough to buy clothes for the children, and her mother scraped and saved and stitched by candlelight, and often looked tired and worn. Somewhere there was injustice. Somewhere the balance had gone. (p. 26)

Who is speaking here? Neither Daphne du Maurier nor her many narrative voices is given to crying out against injustice to women. Has Mary Anne leaped out of the past, like the ancestors George du Maurier dreamed of, to protest, using her great-great-granddaughter as medium? Is Daphne du Maurier cunningly adjusting her rhetoric to fit an earlier England in which the idiom of protest was available to women, a prerogative that had vanished by 1954? This free-floating denunciation of innate male incapacity and endowed male power is the essence of du Maurier's vision, but only *Mary Anne* makes that vision explicit. The novelist masks herself; the ancestor speaks plainly.

This strong feminist awareness is the guiding spirit of *Mary Anne*. I wish I could assert that Daphne du Maurier had found her authentic literary stance in embracing the ancestor who was also her lover: *Mary Anne* is dedicated to two women, to Mary Anne Clarke herself and to "Gertrude Lawrence, who was to have acted the part on the stage." But though *Mary Anne* is not the prosaic story Sophie Duval makes of *The Glass-Blowers*, it is surprisingly schematic. Du Maurier is usually a curt and cryptic novelist. Her resolutions become increasingly, tantalizingly irresolute the more one examines them. Mary Anne's story, however, is uncharacteristically framed in lessons. Each episode teaches her something about the game a woman must play in a man-made world, but since she has known that game from her childhood, a story that is inherently fascinating flattens into monotonous repetition.

Du Maurier may be adopting what she thinks of as the didacticism of Victorian fiction (Mary Anne Clarke lived until 1852), or perhaps when her inheritance finally gives her license to speak out, her message drowns her story. But with all its flatness, *Mary Anne* is so determinedly free of commercial titillation, and yet so unlike du Maurier's other novels, that it is surely the story she believed her great-great-grandmother wanted told. Once again, du Maurier's integrity as a researcher testifies to the authenticity of her family chronicle. The novelist refuses to add spice or sympathy.

Toward the end of the novel, Mary Anne Clarke's stories make her the most famous woman in England: she writes the sordid truth, not only about her lover the duke of York, but about the men in the opposition who try to use her as their political tool. The duke pays her not to publish her story—the annuity that supported George du Maurier's parents for years—but, like George's own Martia in *The Martian*, she seems to call out at the end to a possible Daphne: "I promised I would not publish a word about myself and the Duke and our life together. But the promise bound only myself, and not my heirs....I find the omission intriguing" (p. 312).

Obediently, as accurately as she can, Daphne finally publishes the story of Mary Anne and the duke. But, just before Mary Anne finally goes too far—she is imprisoned for libel and exiled from England—she articulates her encompassing literary mission: to expose powerful men. Her wily mentor spurs her on: "You don't realise the power you have in your pen, and for that matter in your tongue as well. Two men fell to disgrace because of you." But Mary Anne is no Trilby; her story is her own, not any man's.

> His suggestion stirred her, excited her. A series of pamphlets attacking her world, the world she had known; once more a chance to prove she was not forgotten, that she still had the power to break a man.
>
> The battle was on again, the *ideé fixe*—men were a race apart to be subjected. She shut herself up in her room and began to write. (p. 358)

Was the exposure and subjection of men the mission of Daphne du Maurier's fiction as well, fiction that is, at its best and most characteristic, so convoluted and disguised that it looks like romance? Imagining a reborn Mary Anne Clarke inspiring her with a mission, as George was inspired by his Martia, Daphne du Maurier wrote best-selling novels rather than polemical pamphlets, but she too exposed powerful, incapable men. As family chronicler, she was as assiduous as Sophie Duval but as irreverent as Mary Anne Clarke, folding into her own novels a subtly self-referential antagonism that wrestled with the great men she perpetuated.

Chronicles of War

The du Maurier households—both that of Daphne's parents and her own—spoke in code. Their code words were usually ways of muffling anything uncomfortable or inadmissible—"menace" meant sexual attraction, "Venetian" meant lesbian, "wain" meant to be embarrassed, indulging in a "tell-him" was to be boring, the cardinal du Maurier sin.[7] In true du Maurier fashion, Daphne the family chronicler told her stories twice: once in her straightforward chronicles, nonfictional or novelized, and then, in her more serious fiction, in code. In her straightforward chronicles, the author disappears, but in the coded chronicles, a menaced figure exudes ancestral apparitions. The explicit chronicles respect the past they resurrect, but in the coded chronicles, ancestral apparitions are dangerous to everyone they meet.

The most powerful apparition in her novels is not, overtly, her father, but the tenderest, most wistful incarnation of her beloved grandfather. The most potent, if hidden, ghost in the haunted *Rebecca* is not that of the lost wife but that of loving, yearning George du Maurier, with his romanticism twisted into hate. *Rebecca*, like *Peter Ibbetson*—and like most of Daphne du Maurier's most effective novels—is a plunge into the past, but for her, the recovered past holds horror.

In *Peter Ibbetson*, the symbol of Mary's restorative capacity is an apple tree. "I shall soon be here again, by this apple-tree; I shall count the hours," she cries rapturously after having taught Peter the art of dreaming true.[8] Mary at the apple tree is the gateway to restoration: through her visionary power, the walls of Peter Ibbetson's prison dissolve. His gratitude to her is a prayer: "You gave me your hand, and all came straight at once. My old school rose in place of the jail" (p. 244). Under Mary's direction, he does find himself back in his happy old school, then back in the garden with his dead parents, who are magically young and beautiful once more, and finally, in the palace of art he and Mary construct in their dream country, a Never Land of aesthetic omnipotence. Through Mary's occult influence, Peter possesses not only a soulmate but also history and art. He is married eternally; time and space are his theater.

Daphne's tale "The Apple Tree" (1952)[9] is a similar parable of a loving woman's restorative power. The sour widower who tells the story always hated his sad and sighing wife. He is horrified when a barren tree in his orchard miraculously flowers, producing bushels of inedible apples; he knows that like *Peter Ibbetson*'s grand Mary, his wretched wife lives again through the tree. The distasteful apples keep coming, but they inspire no husbandly exaltation, no time travel, no palace of art—only guilty revulsion. This resurrection tale, if it is one, escalates into an account of the mutual murder that defines the marriages in Daphne du Maurier's fiction.

When she transplants conjugal resurrection to a novel, the less allegorical and more developed *Rebecca,* it is a still more lethal restoration. The naive narrator begins with a *Peter Ibbetson*-like wish: "If only there could be an invention . . . that bottled up a memory, like scent. And it never faded, and it never got stale. And then, when one wanted it, the bottle could be uncorked, and it would be like living the moment all over again."[10]

George du Maurier's Peter Ibbetson and his Mary had already lived the invention for which *Rebecca*'s narrator yearns to her bane. As Peter rhapsodizes: "our greatest pleasure of all was to live our old life over again and again, and make Gogo and Mimsey [their childhood selves] and our parents and cousins and M. le Major go through their old paces once more" (p. 327).

In *Rebecca*, though, the old life returns to strangle, for the past is domestic murder, and Rebecca, who like the wife in "The Apple Tree" refuses to die, is its spirit. The invention that uncorks bottled-up memory materializes when the gullible narrator wears Rebecca's former costume to the Manderley fancy dress ball. The costume conjures both the ancestral de Winters and Rebecca herself, who brilliantly simulated those ancestors, but this pageant of the past releases rage and disaster: resurrections are set in motion until Rebecca's body rises out of the sea, exposing her lordly husband as the murderer he is in his heart. In *Peter Ibbetson*, marriage is communion with the ancestral past. For Daphne du Maurier, forgetting, not memory, is conjugal grace.

When Rebecca returns to the Manderley that never forgot her, she arouses in her husband a hate that focuses on George du Maurier's most renowned object of love: her foot. In *Trilby*, the true lover Little Billee immortalizes Trilby's grand foot by drawing it on a wall—a Cinderella-like tribute so romantic in the 1890s that it inspired hosts of foot-shaped commodities. But for *Rebecca*'s Maxim de Winter, his wife's foot is a maddening inducement to murder. He remembers with fury "that foot of hers, swinging to and fro, that damned foot in its blue and white striped sandal," whose defiant motion leads him to kill her (p. 279). In Daphne du Maurier's world, there can be no foot-shaped ice creams or other delectable foods. Memory is indeed bottled like scent, but when uncorked, it unleashes a hatred too unsavory for public consumption.

Trilby was so loved that it was not enough for Victorian audiences to read it over and over, to see it on the stage, to relish its characters through the author's own illustrations, to eat rich food in the shape of the heroine's foot; in some strange communion, Englishmen took to wearing the novel on their heads in the shape of a soft felt homburg that mysteriously came to be called a "trilby hat," though no such hat is featured in du Maurier's novel. Trilby hats bob through Daphne's later tales like a sinister joke; invariably they portend disaster.

"The Little Photographer"[11] concerns a spoiled marquise ground into petulant despair by the inanition of her life as a wealthy wife. She has nothing to do but to take a lover, so she selects the crippled photographer of the title. At first he is suitably deferential; it is only when she notices his "cheap trilby hat" that he turns sinister. Like the woman by the apple tree, the man in the trilby hat is the gateway, not to rapture, but to mutual murder.

In "Ganymede," a jolly man in a trilby hat becomes the story's Satan. A shy classical scholar travels to Venice, where he falls in love with a beautiful waiter. Certain that the waiter is Ganymede incarnate, trembling on the brink of visionary transformation, he is devastated by a dreadful specter: "I saw a large man in a white raincoat and a broad-brimmed trilby hat step out from the shadows beneath the colonnade and tap him on the shoulder. My boy raised his head and smiled. In that brief moment I experienced evil. A premonition of disaster."[12] Like that of all Daphne du Maurier narrators, his sense of disaster is infallible: "Ganymede," like "The Little Photographer," ends in murder and ruination.

In the same collection, the sweetly respectable painter in "The Alibi"—whose modest demeanor and hidden rage for power evoke George du Maurier himself—announces his murderous ordinariness by his hat. "The effort to size him up was beyond her [his prospective victim]—the tweed suit, appropriate for London or the country, the trilby hat, the walking stick, the fresh-complexioned face, the forty-five to fifty years" (p. 17). This sweet man seems so Britishly banal that he defies categorization, but we have shared his thoughts: "The impulse was strong within him to say, 'I have come to strangle you. You and your child. I bear you no malice whatever. It just happens that I am the instrument of fate sent for this purpose.' Instead, he smiled" (p. 16). Even without this blatant self-proclamation, his trilby hat is, in the author's family code, a sufficient declaration of butchery. Mementos of her grandfather's beloved book are Daphne du Maurier's messengers of doom.

The woman at the apple tree, the swinging foot, the trilby hats, all those reminders of her grandfather that weave through her works—especially the tales, more private and elliptical than the novels—are portents of death, but whose, and why? Does the sentimental old Victorian murder by his nature the brittle modern woman simply because he was open, expansive, in tune with his times? Or were his romantic fantasies always murderous to the woman who waited by the apple tree, the girl whose foot became ice cream and whose voice melted into a thwarted old man's fantasy? True to her coded upbringing, Daphne du Maurier simultaneously indicted her grandfather's romantic vision, relived it, and endowed it with a power the old man never believed he had.

Her splendid, largely overlooked novel, *The House on the Strand* (1969), is her darkest and most mordant revision of her grandfather's yearning to regress. Like Peter Ibbetson, the narrator is a time traveler who lives a double life; with the help of an equivocal male guide (not the grand affirming Mary) and an LSD-like drug "that turned a clear brain sick"[13] (not the godlike mental powers cultivated by that elect spirit Peter Ibbetson), Dick Young escapes his dismal wife to visit the fourteenth century in visions. But though he tries to belong to the past, the increasingly estranged Dick is a ghost in both the present and antiquity.

In *The House on the Strand*, the relation between past and present is dissonant and mad, while in *Peter Ibbetson*, that union progressed to perfection. In *Peter Ibbetson*, Mary initially warns Peter that the past, like theater, can be seen but never touched: "And mind, also, you must take care how you touch things or people—you may hear, and see, and smell; but you mustn't touch, nor pick flowers or leaves, nor move things about. It blurs the dream, like breathing on a window-pane. I don't know why, but it does" (p. 209). Magnus, Dick's guide in *The House on the Strand*, gives advice identical to Mary's but more fearful: "If you meet a figure from the past, don't for heaven's sake touch him. Inanimate objects don't matter, but if you try to make contact with living flesh the link breaks, and you'll come to with a very unpleasant jerk. I tried it: I know" (p. 11).

Peter Ibbetson, whose journey into the past is a progress, does learn to touch an infallibly caressing past and even to participate in it: "Soon I discovered by practice that I was able for a second or two to be more than a mere spectator—to be an actor once more; to turn myself (Ibbetson) into my old self (Gogo), and thus be touched and caressed by those I had so loved.... Moreover, I soon learned to touch things without sensibly blurring the dream" (p. 232).

For Peter's tormented descendant, who is increasingly consumed by his visions, the journey between present and past is more and more blurred. By the end, Dick is trapped in opposing worlds, both of which erode him. "The house was inhabited not by the dead but by the living, and I was the restless wanderer, I was the ghost," he realizes on one of his final odysseys (p. 263); the house he refers to exists simultaneously in his lost past and lost present. As Dick decomposes, reality and dream become interchangeably violent and doom-ridden.

Clinical rather than tender, Daphne du Maurier turns her

grandfather's myth of redemption, and of noble medieval ancestors, into an account of madness, rage, and the impossibility of escape. The violence and terror within her gentle grandfather's backward yearning, and within the excruciating nostalgia of J. M. Barrie, who wrote such wonderful parts for her father, ruthlessly decompose in *The House on the Strand.*

Daphne du Maurier gave birth to three children, but she was, in her own mind, daughter and granddaughter, never mother: she defined herself as legatee rather than ancestor. Her acknowledged discomfort as a mother sounds brave today, when, publicly at least, and whether or not they have actual children, woman writers are pressured to display maternal credentials in order to authenticate their literary vision. Daphne du Maurier was probably part of the last generation of a female tradition in which maternal emotions were optional, while the business of maternity could be coolly delegated to servants;[14] motherhood, actual or metaphoric, had not yet become the touchstone of womanly authenticity that it is even in the eyes of many feminists today. Morally, I can't regret the passing of the British servant class, but I do envy the blithe indifference to nurturing that Daphne du Maurier expressed so freely. Women today may be less deferential to men, in America at least, but we are forced into a stereotyped femininity that inhibits, in art and in our lives, the daring ontological flexibility of a Daphne du Maurier.

But she too is paying a price. I suspect that her discomfort with motherhood, her self-perception as heir rather than as endower, has made her fiction less accessible to readers today. She was, as a writer, the end of a line: her mission was, as she saw it, to perpetuate the men in her life, and she did, but at the same time she exposed the feebleness of those men and the danger of the worlds they made. Her punishment for seeing so much is the fragility of her own legacy. Daphne du Maurier is both famous and unknown: this proud inheritor of a great tradition, who, when she was most intense and felt most herself, played a male role, is labeled a feminine writer of escapist romance.

Though George du Maurier's characters crop up again and again in her fiction, her father seems scarcely present. He does play some sort of role in *The Parasites* as "Pappy" Delaney, famous singer and head of a beautiful theatrical brood. Pappy is a superb performer, but unlike the Gerald of Daphne's less familial biography, he is known only by his child-talk name. Like Gerald, Pappy falls into terrified infantilism as he ages, but Pappy's decay is emotionally motivated: his irreplaceable wife has suddenly died, while Gerald lost none of the caretaking women he collected.

Pappy may look like Gerald, but he is no actor-manager. Instead of creating himself in all his self-divisions, as Gerald did, he is a creature of George du Maurier, for in his greatest moment he reverts to Trilby. George du Maurier's victim/goddess is at her most overwhelming when she sings the nursery rhyme "Au Claire de la Lune" in three different modes. The narrator rhapsodizes at length about the wealth her voice extracts from a common song: "If she had spread a pair of large white wings and gracefully fluttered up to the roof and perched upon the chandelier, she could not have produced a greater sensation. The like of that voice has never been heard, nor ever will be again. A woman archangel might sing like that, or some enchanted princess out of a fairy tale."[15]

At a key moment in *The Parasites*, Pappy too sings "Au Clair de la Lune" to similarly rhapsodic effect, though his son's analytic perspective adds a characteristically sharp descriptive edge:

> Pappy used to sing this for a final encore very often. The simpler the song, the wilder became the audience. They would scream, and wave handkerchiefs, and stamp with their feet— just because he did nothing at all but stand perfectly still on the stage and sing a little simple song [just as Trilby did] that everybody had learnt in their cradle. It was the voice going soft that did it—you got the same effect with a muted string on a fiddle. And, more exciting still, you could get the same sadness out of "Mon ami Pierrot" by changing the notes around; the melody was the same and the general sense, but by changing the chords,

the note of despair became sharper. It was even more exciting to play the melody to a different time.[16]

When she suffused Pappy in Trilby, Daphne gave her father less agency than he had in his theatrical life, but she restored, perhaps, an artistic power lacking in the seductive player of double men.

The Parasites is autobiographical fantasy, not autobiographical fiction: unlike Gerald, Pappy marries an artistic partner rather than a fussing wife, a radiant, Isadora Duncan-like dancer who defiantly, unconventionally, dances alone, and whose death takes the light out of the family. So unique a woman, so committed an artist, would have been too much for her needy father. Pappy is Gerald without his timidity and conventionality, that is, the Gerald who might have been.

"The Menace," a late story (1959), might be an expressionist portrait of Gerald, though its medium is not the theater but the films Gerald hated. The Menace of the title is a tough movie star who looks like Humphrey Bogart, not her handsome father. Like Gerald's love scenes, though, his hostile onscreen lovemaking is seductively shorn of desire:

> Barry Jeans the Menace really started the fashion that became so prevalent between the two wars on both sides of the Atlantic of men and women not making love at all. What was vulgarly called "making a pass" was no longer done. If a fellow took a girl home in his car, and drew up in front of his house, there was no question of parking and staying put for half an hour. Barry Jeans never did that. He pulled the trilby hat still further over his eyes, his mouth became more stern, and he said something like "Quit…" The next thing you saw was the girl on the front doorstep, fitting a key in the lock and crying, and Barry Jeans banking the corner in his Cadillac.[17]

As usual, the trilby hat is a portent of doom, but its murderousness is subtler than that of "The Alibi" or "Ganymede": we learn in the course of the story that this infantile idol can be stimulated only by incessant mothering. Just as his career is fading, he meets a nanny-like woman from his past who takes such bustling, sexless care of him that he continues to exude sex appeal on the screen.

Pappy may be Gerald at his grandest; the Menace may be Gerald stripped to his essential nature. In reality, though, Daphne du Maurier continued to write and revise her father's biography, for, whether they are heroic or cringing, all her men live multiple lives; all are in thrall to some tutelary man from whom they cannot separate; and, since her novels realize the impulses her father had buried, all her men are murderers of women.

Her theatrical woman-killers pervaded by controlling doubles are not, of course, Gerald du Maurier, but they do transmute into twentieth-century psychological horror the radiant Edwardian actor-manager who acted out his own father's compelling fantasies; who, to show off his virtuosity, played Mr. Darling as well as Captain Hook; whose gentleman-criminals made him a theatrical exemplar of a double life; who demanded so much mothering that he crammed his life with women. Daphne du Maurier's male-centered novels of inheritance give her magnanimous father his most torn and tragic roles.

4

Life as a Man

The few critics who pay attention to Daphne du Maurier consign her to a feminine ghetto, declaring *Rebecca* her crowning and most characteristic achievement, but for me, her finest and most characteristic novels appear indifferent to female, feminine, or even feminist fantasies or realities. *I'll Never Be Young Again, The Progress of Julius, My Cousin Rachel, Hungry Hill, The Scapegoat, The Flight of the Falcon,* and *The House on the Strand,* as well as her novelized biographies *Gerald* and *The Infernal World of Branwell Brontë,* are all stories about men told from within. The powerful impersonations in *Hungry Hill* and *The Scapegoat* first drew me to her work, making me perhaps the only admirer of Daphne du Maurier who did not read *Rebecca* first—or at least the only one who admits it.

Something about this group of novels embarrasses even du Maurier devotees. Perhaps these male-centered novels are off-putting because they are so good: a brilliant performer, du Maurier makes us believe in and live with her terrified, violent non-heroes. Generally, even the best woman novelists play men with an undercurrent of self-conscious parody: the male narrators of Charlotte Brontë's *Professor* and George Eliot's *Adam Bede* signal their manliness by strutting and posturing. In our own century, Edith Wharton's *Age of Innocence* and *Ethan Frome*, both told from a male perspective, are, compared to Daphne du Maurier's novels, point-making constructions of shadowy heroes or anti-heroes.[1] Daphne du Maurier's male-centered group of novels makes the immersed reader forget that the author is a woman.

Daphne du Maurier had good reason to identify with men. Her family being what it was, talent was passed through the paternal line. Despite the fiat of her contemporary Virginia Woolf that we as women "think back through our mothers,"[2] many women don't. Since, among the du Mauriers, women thought incessantly of the men in their care and scarcely at all of their daughters, the loyalty Woolf exhorted women writers to feel would have been wasted on Daphne, who was, moreover, the heir designate from childhood. While her mother and grandmother perfected stylish subordination, no one thought such deference appropriate for the talented, sullen Daphne. Even her lovely hybrid name is, like Virginia Woolf's name, a bequest from gifted, successful males. In Daphne du Maurier's case, thinking back through her fathers brought treasure and fruitful terror; thinking back through her mothers would have meant renouncing thought.

Moreover, she had a passionate self within her self: the boy in the box, that independent entity who fell in love with women while preserving the wife and mother—the incipient "Lady Browning" and "Dame Daphne du Maurier"—from the tarnish of lesbianism. Today, of course, that boy in the box is a minefield of bad politics and shamed self-repudiation, but like so many components of Daphne du Maurier's private mythology, he affirms an abundance of selves. As she goes on to define him, the boy in the box is a "half-breed" who is also Peter Pan, if a more fragile Peter than Barrie's: "And then the boy realized he had to grow up, and not be a boy any longer, so he turned into a girl, and not an unattractive one at that, and the boy was locked in a box forever."[3] But of course he burst out in the middle of Daphne's life.

The boy in (and out of) the box has little relation to our contemporary ritual of "coming out of the closet." The latter activity is, ideally at least, a confessional release of a sole, authentic, undivided self; the boy in the box is an other self, one who loves, and writes, independently of the wife, the mother, the Lady, the Dame. He is a fractured remnant of childhood, a foreign sexuality, a strange muse.

Du Maurier's fiction about lesbianism is murky and guarded, but inevitably—unlike the fatalism of *The Well of Loneliness*—it involves willed transfiguration. Her novella *Monte Verità* is an allegorical and abstract account of metamorphosis.[4] Anna, an aspiring woman we see only through the eyes of two men who love her, abandons her husband to join a rarefied community of women on a mountaintop. This Shangri-la generates undefined transformations that unnerved du Maurier's publisher Victor Gollancz: "I don't understand the slight implication that there is something wrong with sex," he wrote plaintively.[5]

In the spirit of transfiguration that governed du Maurier, Anna was originally supposed to turn into a boy, but this upset Gollancz so much that Anna became a leper instead. Du Maurier's uncharacteristic compliance suggests that it scarcely mattered to her what Anna turned into: the point was becoming another self. From one point of view, the boy in the box and other metamorphic eruptions are self-hating symptoms from an unenlightened time, but unlike the "real" self who comes out of the closet, they allowed Daphne du Maurier to explode into another being.

She was, after all, an actor's daughter, though in Gerald du Maurier's day, no Actors Studio trained performers to reach into their depths. The movie stars of his day were as mercurial as stage performers; film acting had not yet settled into the understated sincerity which demands that actors exude their own essences (or seem to) rather than playing roles. For Gerald and his generation, acting was simulating.

In his best roles, he played players who themselves acted their lives, secreting, as Daphne would, a hidden self with a separate role. For Daphne, this insincerity defined art. She remembered her disappointment when her father took off his makeup: "Pity, though, I sometimes thought. He looked nicer with it on, bolder, somehow, and his eyes very bright. Still, it was all part of the game of make-believe that was his, and ours as well. Life was pretending to be someone else. Otherwise it was rather dull."[6]

Even fathers not her own became true, freeing fathers when they turned into someone else. Her biography of Branwell Brontë imagines a father who made his children bold by putting masks on them and even, perhaps, on himself: "Here was Papa yet not Papa. Here was a creature who, concealed behind the grinning head, could turn himself to giant or bogy, inducing tremors of excitement which, because they were frightening, were delicious too."[7] An ideal father, one worthy of artists, is never himself.

Pretending to be someone else is not as juvenile a definition of life as it may sound in today's public rhetoric of confessional sincerity. Many of us do it automatically every day. This apparent pretense is the heart of Daphne du Maurier's life and her art and the great achievement of the family chronicle that comprises her most innovative fiction.

Her male-centered novels are characteristically versatile; they differ from each other in plot, setting, tone, and characters. The men in these novels are not the cloudy, overbearing types of her woman-centered romances, *Jamaica Inn*, *Rebecca*, and *Frenchman's Creek*; they are sharply delineated individuals who could never be mistaken for one another. But their multiple stories are variations on a theme. All her fragile protagonists are bound to an elusive male leader; all are implicated in the death of a woman.

These novels about the torments of interdependent men are not biographies; they are, I think, coded family chronicles. As she made her love affairs into a myth of transfiguration, so she wove her male ancestors into her personal myth. From one point of view, this myth is an exposé, for it is a story of neediness that turns into madness, of a bond sealed, in every case, by a woman's murder. When she makes of the great men homicidal infants, she fulfills the mission she attributed to her great-great-grandmother Mary Anne Clarke: "The battle was on again, the *ideé fixe*—men were a race apart to be subjected. She shut herself up in her room and began to write."[8] Writing is an instrument of power, the best available to a smart woman, whereby heroes are exposed as lechers and liars—and, for Daphne du Maurier if not for the more thick-skinned Mary Anne, as killers as well.

But at the same time as they expose, these male-centered novels embrace her ancestors by becoming them. Her submergence in her male creations is intense enough to constitute a literary version of the incestuous fantasy with which all three du Mauriers flirted, but it is an incest that is strangely detached, an escape from intimacy rather than its consummation.

Convinced that like a good Freudian daughter she harbored incestuous longings, Daphne du Maurier wove incest into her fiction. Characteristically, though, that incest is most piquant when it precludes familiarity or even family. *The Parasites* (1949), her only novel that approaches direct family portraiture, involves the entanglements among the three children of the glamorous theatrical Delaneys. But they are not true siblings; they are the children of different liaisons. Maria and Niall, beautiful, mercurial artists, are the incestuous pair, though they are technically unrelated: dangerously lovable, they can love only each other. Celia, the legitimate child and good daughter, is a lumpish nurturer, as parasitic in her caretaking as Maria and Niall are in their careless artistry. Incest in *The Parasites* is more an escape from family—as embodied by pious Celia—than it is a domestic embrace.

Du Maurier's next novel, *My Cousin Rachel* (1951), is, as the title reminds us, technically about incest: after Ambrose marries his cousin Rachel and dies, the narrator, Philip, another cousin and Ambrose's adopted heir, falls in love with her, is or isn't poisoned by her, and finally murders her. But despite the title, there is nothing familial about Rachel. She is utterly foreign: not only was she raised in Italy, but she is a woman, "a race apart" to these ingrown men. Like Daphne du Maurier's boy in the box, Rachel is mystery, surprise, possible danger, possible transfiguring honesty. Ambrose and Philip love each other because they know each other; they love Rachel because she is all they will never know.

The tortuous novella *A Border-Line Case* (1971) depicted incest explicitly enough to shock readers when it appeared, but here too incest is aroused by mystery and distance.[9] When her beloved father dies, Shelagh, the narrator, a gutsy young actress, drives to Ireland to meet the satanically named Nick, her father's naval friend from whom he had become mysteriously estranged. Nick is one of the exhalations of romance who inhabit du Maurier's woman-centered stories: he lives mysteriously on a ship docked off a remote island, he commands stalwart men, he is a dedicated archeologist of prehistoric Irish artifacts and an equally devoted Irish terrorist.

Nick is no father figure but instead a variant of the pirate-aesthete who ravished the lady in du Maurier's popular romance *Frenchman's Creek*: he exudes sexy strangeness. Only after their affair is over does Shelagh realize that he is indeed her father: when she is opening in *Twelfth Night*, Nick sends her an old photograph of himself in the same play, also starring as Viola/Cesario. She recognizes her own face in his, finding her father, not in any home, but in a romance of shared simulated boyhood.

Du Maurier's supposedly incestuous love stories have the facade of family but the lure of distance. They resemble George du Maurier's familial non-family in *Peter Ibbetson*, whose lovers grow up together, live together, and encounter a common ancestor in dreams while remaining separated in their waking existence: as with Shelagh and Nick, or the lady and the pirate, their love story is defined by division. The du Maurier dream of incest is a dream of an impossible union that is at the same time an escape from family life.

There is nothing domestic about the family myth that underlies Daphne du Maurier's most haunting and imaginative fiction, a myth that first appears in an overwrought apprentice work. The melodramatic *I'll Never Be Young Again* (1932), du Maurier's second novel, lays out the plot. Dick, du Maurier's first male narrator, is a bilious young man who moves from a passionate friendship with Jake to a sadistic love affair with Hesta. The friendship is all-embracing; the love affair is inchoate and tormented. In this novel, it is Jake, the male double, who dies, while Hesta merely sinks into debauchery. Nevertheless, this early work establishes du Maurier's central paradigm of intimacy between men, but murderousness between men and women.

Her third novel, *The Progress of Julius* (1933), inaugurates her male plot full-blown and blatant. Her later novels would tell the ugly story of Julius elliptically and discreetly, but not differently.

Like George du Maurier, Julius Lévy is a French émigré who becomes wealthy in England, but Julius's Paris is the rotting underbelly of the city that George represented as gently cherishing and tragically lost, a treasure box of parents, comrades, art, play. The Paris of *The Progress of Julius* is a catastrophic site, blasted by siege and crushing defeat in the Franco-Prussian War, events undreamed-of in George du Maurier's pre-Imperial boyhood under the monarch he affectionately called "the bourgeois king." The Paris that haunts Daphne's Julius smashes her grandfather's dream.

Just as George's dream city becomes, a generation later, Julius's nightmare, George's charm dissipates into Julius's avarice. Daphne memorialized her grandfather as a conduit of love: "He radiated a kind of warmth that made people turn to him on sight with sympathy, and as they came to know him better this quality of warmth caught at their hearts, just as his novels caught at his readers'."[10] Julius, an unsavory (and unpleasantly stereotyped) Jewish businessman, radiates hunger and hate.[11]

George du Maurier caught hearts; Julius captures appetites. The stuff of his prosperity is not delicious drawings and books but the food that composes his economic empire. As a child, he sells vegetables at the market Les Halles with his gargantuan grandfather. After Prussian soldiers shoot this sheltering grandpère and the siege of Paris begins, Julius sells rats to his starving countrymen. He emigrates to Algeria, then to England, where he works for a baker and buys his employer out, thus beginning the huge success of his cheap restaurant chains. His ambition articulates the aim of the invader who haunts du Maurier's fiction: "I'll put a chain around England that nobody will break."[12]

The food that envelops both England and the novel is an unusually sensuous ingredient in Daphne du Maurier's work; her later men will inspire, and be consumed by, more impalpable hungers. The novel engulfs us sickeningly in food, but this food, which we can never quite taste, seems an abstract transplantation from the oppressively physical world of Emile Zola, especially *Le Ventre de Paris* (1872), Zola's novel about Les Halles, the overpowering creation of his hated Napoleon III. For Zola, the market is the loathsome center of Imperial Paris: "The stomach—Paris's stomach, Les Halles, where food pours in before flowing out to various neighborhoods. Humanity's stomach and by extension the bourgeoisie munching, digesting, peacefully ruminating its joys and flaccid morals."[13]

The food that seems to swallow *The Progress of Julius* is reminiscent of Zola, as is the detail with which du Maurier describes Julius's business enterprises: if we wanted to build up a chain of restaurants, this novel would tell us how to do it, though her later books take only cursory interest in details of commerce.

Du Maurier never acknowledged Zola. Her autobiography pays fulsome tribute to Katherine Mansfield but ignores the impact on her of great men like Zola or Thomas Mann, with whose work her fiction is clearly suffused; in fact, she scarcely mentions her grandfather's novels in depth, though she writes at length about his life. Imaginatively, she had no compunctions about becoming a man, but she presented herself publicly as segregated in a female tradition. As she defined herself, she was an exemplary woman writer who learned from women alone.

Accordingly, the food in *The Progress of Julius* has none of the broad cultural circulation of the food sold at Zola's Les Halles. In this novel, hunger is a mere route to money; money is a route to power; and power is a means of sating the true hunger of du Maurier's men—the need to murder their women.

In the course of his story, Julius murders, directly or obliquely, four women—five if we count his beloved cat, Mimitte, whom, as a little boy fleeing the Prussian invaders, he drowns so that no one else will have her. Shortly thereafter, still a child, he watches approvingly as his gentle father murders his adulterous mother. "It served Mère right. She deserved to die after going with Jacques Tripet. He could understand why Père had killed her. He didn't want his thing to be spoilt. He would not allow anyone else to have it" (p. 47). In the course of his rise, for no strong reason, he kills or lets die his mistress, his wife, and his daughter in turn. He ends the novel in grotesque isolation, forlorn, like Orson Welles's Citizen Kane, among the treasures he amassed, but though he misses his father and his power, he seems scarcely to remember his women.

Julius's minutely analyzed sadism develops independently of his restaurant empire. He gains nothing by torturing women but pleasure:

> He had discovered a new thing, of hurting people he liked. It gave him an extraordinary sensation to see Elsa cry after she had been smiling, and to know that he had caused her tears. He was aware of power, strange and exciting. In a way it was like the desire to make love. The two longings were very close together. To say something bitter and cruel, to watch the smile fade from Elsa's lips and the shadows come into her eyes, to taunt her until she put her hands over her face, it made his heart beat and his blood race the same as when he held her and loved her. (p. 96)

Here, in coarse and explicit form, is the motive that drives du Maurier's more genteel—and gentile—killers of women, Maxim de Winter, of *Rebecca,* and Philip Ashley, of *My Cousin Rachel.*

This ugly story is so far from the Daphne du Maurier of popular stereotype, its ferocity seems so close to anti-Semitism, that most lovers of du Maurier pretend *The Progress of Julius* doesn't exist.[14] There are indeed suggestions that Julius's misogyny is part of his developing self-awareness as a Jew. His first visit to an Orthodox synagogue moves him because the women are segregated ("He smiled to himself, it was just, it was right. Instinctively he approved of this. Creatures apart" [p. 40]); his wife-killing father is the sweet soul of Jewish patriarchy.

But from the beginning of her career, Daphne du Maurier's men killed women with little discernible motive and made the reader live with them. "Panic," the first early story she published in *The Rebecca Notebook* (pp. 47-55), is a lurid account, from the male perspective, of a man who kills his childlike lover during their Paris liaison. Another early story features a self-absorbed actor, clearly based on her father. Pretending to remember a former lover, he smothers her in romantic clichés, but another self slips out: "Then, because I loved you so much, I'd want to strangle you, and…" (*Rebecca Notebook*, p. 103). These suave protagonists of little-known stories are far from Jewish, but as with Julius, killing is their climax of love.

Like Svengali, Julius Lévy is an exotic personification of a common male instinct gone mad—the desire to possess women and control them. Daphne du Maurier's unappetizing Jews are mirrored in her equally unsavory English gentlemen. Nothing in her novels equals the abrupt and vicious anti-Semitic outburst in her grandfather's supposedly lovable *Peter Ibbetson*:

> To pray for any personal boon or remission of evil…was in my eyes simply futile; but, putting its futility aside, it was an act of servile presumption, of wheedling impertinence, not without suspicion of a lively sense of favors to come.
>
> It seemed to me as though the Jews—a superstitious and business-like people, who know what they want and do not care how they get it—must have taught us to pray like that.
>
> It was not the sweet, simple child innocently beseeching that to-morrow might be fine for its holiday, or that Santa Claus would be generous; it was the cunning trader, fawning, flattering, propitiating, bribing with fulsome, sycophantic praise (an insult in itself), as well as burnt-offerings, working for his own success here and hereafter, and his enemy's confounding.

It was the grovelling of the dog, without the dog's single-hearted love, stronger than even its fear or its sense of self-interest.

What an attitude for one whom God had made after His own image—even towards his Maker![15]

Nothing in *The Progress of Julius* resembles this rabid isolating of "the Jews," whose very prayers contaminate "us." In George du Maurier's novels, Jews are lone monsters. No Englishman could be as potently perverse as *Trilby*'s Svengali, for his power of mesmeric possession comes from another world, "the mysterious East! The poisonous East—birthplace and home of an ill wind that blows nobody good."[16] This epitome of foreignness contaminates Trilby not only by infusing his music into her mouth; when Trilby O'Ferrall metamorphoses into La Svengali, he turns the strapping Irish girl into a Jew.

Daphne's Jews are as European as George du Maurier was: Julius, too, is a product of Paris, not "the mysterious East." There is nothing occult about him. Little but his poverty separates him from Daphne du Maurier's English landowners and lovers. "Something for nothing," the obsessed motto of the ambitious young man, is not only the grating stereotype of an avaricious Jew, it is also, implicitly, the motto of du Maurier's possessive gentry. Maxim de Winter in *Rebecca*, Philip Ashley in *My Cousin Rachel*, Jean de Gué in *The Scapegoat*, all demand without giving, yearning murderously to possess something for nothing.

Du Maurier's best-known slaughtered women have suggestively Jewish names. There are two murdered Rachels in her work: the wife in *The Progress of Julius* is Rachel, making her an implicit foreshadowing of the more equivocal Contessa Rachel Sangaletti (or Mrs. Rachel Ashley) in *My Cousin Rachel*. And of course there is oddly named Rebecca, seemingly the flower of Anglo wifehood, perfect hostess, perfect chatelaine, perfect lady of the manor. The two Rachels, both of whom are praised as intelligent but properly subservient,[17] and the grand Rebecca bring Jewishness into the heart of England. By giving her most womanly women Jewish names, du Maurier reminds us that even the most pliant women are strangers, vulnerable to slaughter. If they have the alien powers of a Svengali, their powers do not save them.

The Progress of Julius is the raw material of Daphne du Maurier's more artful novels; her work becomes, not less violent, but more controlled. As with her grandfather's Svengali, the supposed primitivism of a Jewish protagonist may have allowed her to represent a possessive ferocity that inhibited Englishmen masked. Julius's tormented jealousy recalls Gerald's. Like the aging Gerald, Julius rages to possess the daughter who reminds him of his lost father; like Daphne perhaps, but anticipating as well the suicidal defiance of Rebecca, Julius's daughter, Gabriel, threatens to marry to escape him. Fatally, she taunts her extraordinary father with her impending conventionality: "You won't recognise me soon. I'll be domesticated and subservient and humble, and talking about chintz curtains and babies' napkins" (p. 298). Helplessly, he drowns her as he had drowned the cat he wanted no one else to own, though Gabriel may collaborate in a sudden suicide that is preferable to domesticated death. There is little to choose here between the Jewish tycoon and Maxim de Winter, the chilly landowner, in their reaction to women's taunting refusals.

Since *Rebecca* is a novel about women, not men, Maxim has no engulfing father to possess him and tell him when to kill. Julius, like Gerald, is the yearning creature of his loving, liquidating paternal inheritance. The tender union of father and son sealed in the murders of their women may be Daphne du Maurier's private parable of her own artistic inheritance, one whose loving paternalism threatened to drown the dynamic daughter.

Her later male-centered novels are as subtle and chilling as anything she wrote. All question not only the bases of guilt and innocence but also the foundations of male identity; the narrators of all lose the boundaries of their being, so possessed are they by an engulfing male double. Nevertheless, these intricate novels take their pattern from the overwrought *Progress of Julius*, for they too embed a woman's murder in an indelible bond between men. The high civilization of *My Cousin Rachel* is scarcely less savage than the lurid milieu of *The Progress of Julius*. In *Rachel*, the siege of Paris, the ravenousness of Jews, are displaced by a romantic young Englishman falling into first love. Julius's violent emigrations modulate, in *Rachel*, into the predictable transmissions of English patriarchy.

Julius is structured around catastrophes; *My Cousin Rachel* is steeped in tradition. Philip Ashley, the sensitive young narrator, embodies English continuity: "I shall become a justice of the peace, as Ambrose was, and also be returned one day to Parliament. I shall continue to be honoured and respected, like all my family before me. Farm the land well, look after the people" (p. 12). But Philip's fealty to the past eats itself. It is not the foreigner Rachel who shatters his life, but his possession by his older cousin and adoptive father, Ambrose. Like so many of du Maurier's men, Ambrose makes the fatal decision to leave England for Italy, where he marries his (and Philip's) enigmatic cousin Rachel and dies suddenly, convinced that Rachel has poisoned him.

Rachel personifies the foreign invader so potent in du Maurier's fiction; when she leaves Italy for England, she devastates Philip, less in herself (a self he, and we, never know) than as a personification of Ambrose's destiny. Philip too falls in love with her, but unlike Ambrose, he survives his passion: unable to marry or possess Rachel, fearing her poison, he kills her. He ends the novel in thrall, not to the dead woman, but to his dead male leader:

> I have become so like [Ambrose] that I could be his ghost.
> …I have wondered lately if, when he died, his mind clouded
> and tortured by doubt and fear, feeling himself forsaken and
> alone in that damned villa where I could not reach him, whether
> his spirit left his body and came home here to mine, taking
> possession, so that he lived again in me, repeating his own mistakes, caught the disease once more and perished twice. It may
> be so. All I know is that my likeness to him, of which I was so
> proud, proved my undoing. (p. 13)

As the near-savage Julius recapitulated his father's murder of his mother, so Philip, in the marriage between men that is the heart of Daphne du Maurier's fiction, relives his cousin's life.

My Cousin Rachel is an eminently Victorian novel, one that goes back beyond the nostalgia of George du Maurier and J. M. Barrie, both of whom were haunted by their own belatedness. Like many mid-Victorian works, it seems to be about a femme fatale, but the woman is a cloudy catalyst for the narrative convolutions of a murderous man.

Like Robert Browning's most famous dramatic monologues, especially "Porphyria's Lover," "My Last Duchess," and "Andrea Del Sarto," those self-loving perorations by men who have literally or figuratively murdered their women (all of which generations of students used to recite with gusto), *My Cousin Rachel* is about respectable woman-murder. Though du Maurier claimed that the novel was about her own unattainable beloved, the impeccable Ellen Doubleday, its title, like that of *Rebecca,* is a red herring; the novel should be called *The Progress of Philip* or *The Ashleys,* drawing us to its male narrator as Browning's poems do. True, the title *My Cousin Rachel* does, in its proprietary rhythm, recall the title "My Last Duchess," and Rachel's sophisticated confidant Rainaldi does slyly find "a Del Sarto touch about" Philip (p. 240),[18] but great men like Robert Browning—or Zola or Mann—never enter du Maurier's pantheon of literary mentors. She was, and is, thought to be a woman's writer, and *My Cousin Rachel* has all the accouterments of a woman's book. But though it abounds in the material of an ironic novel that Rachel herself might write, that of a Continental sophisticate enmeshed in the fantasies of two misogynist British landowners, Rachel never tells her story.

The novel is Victorian not only in its emphasis on a femme fatale who disappears into the torn perceptions of her lovers; it is primarily a novel about Victorian men. The story is apparently set in nineteenth-century England, but it contains even fewer historic markers than *Rebecca*—costume, ideology, mode of travel, the British obsession with Italy as its own Gothic mirror,[19] give no insistent period definition; du Maurier locates an essentially Victorian story in an indeterminate age. Its seemingly timeless action could occur in 1850 or in 1950.

Rachel, its opaque female center, is a more tactful descendant of Thackeray's witty foreigner Becky Sharp. Becky too is penniless, flexible, and clever, sidling into the fantasies of the men who think they have captured her. At the climax of her story, Becky dissolves into a question mark in the moral muttering of the gentleman-narrator: "What *had* happened? Was she guilty or not? She said not; but who could tell what was truth which came from those lips; or if that corrupt heart was in this case pure?"[20] Similarly, Rachel ends not as a character but as an indeterminate verdict: the bereft Philip wanders through his estate wondering, "Was Rachel innocent or guilty?" (p. 12).

This fictional autobiography of an Englishman, Victorian in his romantic rage to possess, his faith in some equation between murder and justice, his assumption that women are the fodder of his psychic torment, finds its best commentary in Daphne du Maurier's extraordinary biography of a real Victorian man: the forlorn, obsessed Patrick Branwell Brontë.

The Infernal World of Branwell Brontë is an account of a Victorian male might-have-been that is so brilliantly analyzed, so vividly realized, that it should put to rest the tired cliché (perpetuated by du Maurier herself) that Daphne du Maurier is the heir of "the Brontës"—meaning, of course, the famous female Brontës, Charlotte and Emily. Unlike each other as they were, Charlotte and Emily Brontë were still more unlike Daphne du Maurier. Her biography of their obscure, untalented, addicted brother ratifies the only legacy that du Maurier's work—if not her publicity—claimed: she is the heir of men alone, even when the men are twisted and insane. In this biography, "the Brontës" (meaning the famous sisters) appear only glancingly, as self-sufficient, rather complacent counterparts to their muddled brother.

This biography is as much case history as literary study. Du Maurier makes no claims for Branwell's talent, though she appears to have doggedly read and thought about his many dreadful poems, the interminable Angrian juvenilia on which he and Charlotte collaborated throughout, and long beyond, their childhood, even his bombastic translations of Horace. The care and penetration of her research puts most American academics to shame, but it never makes her fall in love with her subject. As with *Gerald*, her empathy with a floundering man is ruthlessly clear-eyed, and as with *Gerald*, she makes the reader want to flee the man she understands so thoroughly.

One of the many books du Maurier lists among Branwell's unwritten works could have been a source for her own lifelong study of powerful men: *Manhood, the Cause of Its Preservation and Decline* (p. 127). Had Branwell written this book, Daphne du Maurier might not have had to tell and retell the same story; she might instead have settled into being the woman writer most people think she always was. Since neither Branwell nor more eminent scholars have been able to tell us what manhood is, how it can be preserved, and why it is seemingly always declining, Daphne du Maurier made it one of her literary missions to trace that decline over and over, though like the rest of us, she never learned its causes. Branwell Brontë—abusive, self-obsessed, helpless, mad—is the bereft quintessence of all the men in her fiction, but he is not a ruthless survivor like Julius Lévy or a wealthy landowner like Philip Ashley. He has gone down in history as a brother, not a father or a husband or any other sort of owner.

Because Branwell owned nothing and no one, he had no woman to kill; when, in du Maurier's biography, the sisters he had once commanded begin to outgrow and elude him, refusing to remain characters in his ongoing fantasy, he loses himself in delusion. For du Maurier, Branwell Brontë was an appropriate biographical subject because he was mad: he was destroyed not by a thwarted love affair, as he and his biographers claimed, but by "his inability to distinguish truth from fiction, reality from fantasy; and who failed in life because it differed from his own 'infernal world'" (p. 10). The Branwell whom du Maurier describes is Philip Ashley shorn of a killable Rachel.

Daphne du Maurier's shrewdest biographical hypothesis concerns the fatal Mrs. Robinson. As Branwell told the story, he and Mrs. Robinson fell in love when he was tutor to her children. After her husband died, his perfidious will forbade her to marry Branwell; without his great love, he collapsed into opium and solipsistic despair. Elizabeth Gaskell, Charlotte's first biographer, accepted the outline of his story, but the author of *My Cousin Rachel* knows the great love was delusion: his wealthy employer had no idea of her role in the continuing fantasy that was his real life. Like his successful sisters, Mrs. Robinson eluded Branwell's compulsive plot. Unable to kill the women who are stronger than he, Branwell folds into death.

The Infernal World of Branwell Brontë is one of du Maurier's most brilliant books, but it is also a cul-de-sac: there is no narrative thrust, for Branwell begins his story in decline, continuing to deteriorate until he dies. Having no dramatic interest in Charlotte, Emily, and Anne, du Maurier elides the devastating impact of his death on the rest of the family. She might have shown that Branwell's death began to kill his sisters, but she cares only about the man's story. As she conceives it, Branwell's life is a du Maurier novel in which the women get away; thus it has nowhere to go. Without a woman to kill, her men evaporate.

Though her Branwell is deprived of the du Maurier plot, he does have the interpenetrating male guide without whom her men cannot live: his father and namesake. The insane tyrant of Elizabeth Gaskell's biography becomes, in Daphne du Maurier's, Branwell's embracing alternative consciousness, one more pervasive even than his sisters. Some of du Maurier's most beautiful writing evokes the beginning and end of Branwell's life, when he and his father share a room: "Branwell the child, asleep in Mr. Brontë's room, the unknowing medium for his father's loneliness and frustration, worked out in fantasy the rebellions of them both, bringing to fruition the dreams and ambitions that had never, would never, achieve reality" (p. 109).

In Daphne du Maurier's last, and strangest, male-centered novels, *The Flight of the Falcon* and *The House on the Strand*, two men act as mediums for each other's inhibited rebellions. Unlike Branwell, these fictional men do have women to kill, but both novels intensify the dilemma of *My Cousin Rachel* and the tragedy of the Brontë men: what happens to the rebellion when its medium is dead—or mad?

In 1957, six years after the appearance of *My Cousin Rachel* and three years before *The Infernal World of Branwell Brontë*, came *The Scapegoat*, du Maurier's first male-centered book in which the boundaries blur and the allotted roles decompose. *The Scapegoat* may seem regressive, even primitive, to sophisticated theorists of fiction. While *My Cousin Rachel* is an exercise in narrative unreliability, a technique we respect because Henry James and other respectable authors refined it, *The Scapegoat* resurrects a convention from the disreputable Victorian theater: a man meets his double, who has the power to blight his life.

Though no one remembers them now, Charles Reade's *Courier of Lyons* and various adaptations of Dumas's *Corsican Brothers* were staples of the Victorian theatrical repertory and scintillating showcases for actors. *The Corsican Brothers* features the mystic bond between long-separated twins. *The Courier of Lyons*, set in revolutionary France, is darker: a genial, respectable man is confused with his criminal double. The good man is abased, excoriated, and almost executed. At the last minute, the villain is apprehended and the hero is scarred but saved; but Victorian audiences knew that in the actual incident, the wrong man was indeed guillotined.

In *A Tale of Two Cities*, Dickens inflated Reade's melodrama into a parable of moral redemption, but in the theater, doubling was a showcase for the versatility of the actor: moral lessons vanished in the spectacle of a flamboyant performer playing antithetical roles. Becoming two different men in one play was the essence of acting.

Yet thoughtful observers may have seen in theatrical display a portent of the fragility of the self: when we watch a single actor in a double role, we applaud him but fear for ourselves. By the end of the nineteenth century, theatrical breadth evolved into protestations of depth; the double became, not the alien invader, but the true man. Robert Louis Stevenson's austere allegory, *The Strange Case of Dr. Jekyll and Mr. Hyde*, popularized the idea that all roles lurk in a single self. By the early twentieth century, when Gerald du Maurier was a star, doubling roles flaunted psychological profundity, not versatility. Like Stevenson's Jekyll/Hyde, Gerald's Arsène Lupin and Raffles were respectable and criminal at once. Only in a children's play, *Peter Pan*, did Gerald's Mr. Darling/Captain Hook, two indisputably separate characters, return to the supposedly less sophisticated Victorian tradition of doubling.

In *The Scapegoat*, Daphne du Maurier followed Barrie and her father back to the days of Victorian wonder and terror. Her cautious English John and wayward French Jean are not two facets of a single man. *The Scapegoat*, like *The Courier of Lyons*, is frightening because its doubled heroes do not contain each other. Jean and John are incompatible men who share a face, a voice, a body. Like the French and English du Maurier inheritances, they cannot join, but they are at war over a destiny.

Returning to the stylization of Victorian theatrical fantasy allowed the boundaries among Daphne du Maurier's men to begin to dissolve. Her earlier male-centered plots depended on genealogical plausibility. In *My Cousin Rachel*, Ambrose is Philip's cousin and patriarchal leader, though a lost one: Philip inherits Ambrose's estate, his England, his wife, his terrors. In *The Scapegoat*, though, Jean de Gué is a tenuous guide. He does give his forlorn English double an identity and an inheritance—an estate, a family, a business—but is it Jean or John who becomes a model governor? Who energizes the women and reconceives the foundry—the good John, or a new man who is John infused with his puppet master Jean, acting, like du Maurier's Patrick Brontë, as the "unknowing medium" of a deadly visionary? Does either make the other a better, or even a different man? Is Jean wiser at the end because John has been a model of right rule? Is John more human because of Jean's bequest? Or have they penetrated each other as a random experiment in permeability?

Though John and Jean play guide in turn, they are at best collaborators in the novel's most significant event: the death of Jean's wretched wife Françoise, the novel's authentic if obscured scapegoat. The death of the wife begins to heal family and estate. Jean and John are poles apart, but neither loves Françoise enough to keep her alive. In fact, both need her dead.

This indeterminate complicity, which each man in turn seems to direct but neither does, may explain the ethic of political collaboration in these novels. In *The Scapegoat*, the attractively human characters, even the heroic martyr Maurice Duval, have collaborated with the Germans during the occupation; only careless and callous Jean de Gué had joined the Resistance.

Similarly, in *The Flight of the Falcon*, du Maurier's next male-centered novel, this one set in Italy, the dangerously egomaniacal Aldo Donati is a Resistance leader, while the narrator with whom we identify, his insecure brother, begins life as an enforced collaborator: as a child, he left town with his loose mother and her German lover waving a Nazi flag.

In Daphne du Maurier's late works, England becomes the invaded country and resistance is no longer alienating. Defiance is necessary if hopeless in "The Birds," for collaboration with an alien species is inconceivable. In *Rule Britannia*, her grim last novel, the United States invades England to turn it into a theme park, but a crusty old actress and her six adopted sons lead a stalwart resistance and expel the Americans—at least for the time being.

It is more than patriotic chauvinism, though, that makes collaboration appealing in occupied France and Italy but not in England. Collaboration—and the dissolution it requires—is the subject of these novels. Collaborators embrace a protean identity that becomes what an occupying presence makes it; resistance involves solitude, individuality, an internal code, all of which are beyond the du Maurier men and their fictional counterparts. In the later male-centered novels, whose guides dissolve, collaboration is the essence of the action. Since the primary action is the murder of a woman, to murder collaboratively is to elevate the rage of the earlier novels—of *The Progress of Julius* and *My Cousin Rachel*—into the anonymity of a cleansing ritual.

The Flight of the Falcon, one of du Maurier's least coherent works, consists almost entirely of ritual. Like *The Scapegoat*, it is a modernist treatment of a Victorian convention: *The Flight of the Falcon*, like *The Corsican Brothers*, unites long-lost brothers who had believed each other dead. In *The Flight of the Falcon*, the interchange is even more indeterminate than the collaboration between Jean and John in *The Scapegoat*, though du Maurier's pious revisions for the American edition tried to drain away her novel's mystery and danger.

At first, Beo, the vacillating narrator, seems about to drown in the charismatic daring of his older brother, Aldo, who is scholar, quasi-Fascist, lover, leader of a crowd of volatile students.[21] Moreover, Ruffano, the home town to which Beo returns, is a tangled trove of family and civic history: Beo is in danger of drowning, not only in his brother, but in his recovered family past, which is also Italy's historical past.[22]

Of course, there is a murder. Beo has seen an old beggar woman who reminds him of Marta, their beloved nurse whom both brothers remember as the antidote to their betraying mother. He fears he is inadvertently responsible for her murder; Aldo diabolically suggests that Beo actually killed her. But as Aldo begins to weaken, the brothers exchange identities: Aldo is revealed to be Marta's illegitimate son, not Beo's older brother and the heir of their distinguished father.

For a time we think *Aldo* murdered Marta, who was about to reveal his shameful origin. But near the end of an elaborate series of plot twists, he claims to have killed Marta only in a figurative and universal sense: "Yes, I killed her . . . but not with a knife—the knife was merciful. I killed her by despising her, by being too proud to accept the fact I was her son. Wouldn't you say that counts as murder?"

Beo responds with his own declaration of guilt:

> "Well," repeated Aldo, "it was murder, wasn't it?"
> I thought no more of his relationship to Marta, but of my own mother who had died of cancer in Turin. When she had scribbled me a line from hospital, I had not answered.
> "Yes," I said, "it was murder. But we're both guilty, and for the same cause."[23]

Once again, two interpenetrating men collaborate in the murder of a woman—their composite mother, an amalgam of caretaker and slut—but here, the murder is so distant from the main action that it is no longer an impulse in which the horrified reader participates. It rises to a symbolic ceremony. Unlike Gabriel Lévy or Rachel Sangaletti Ashley, these mothers play no role in the novel: they exist to preserve by their deaths the wavering contours of manhood. Murder is no longer pathological; it is archetypal and therapeutic.

Finally, and improbably, Aldo and Beo sacrifice themselves for each other. In the last of a series of esoteric ceremonies, Aldo assumes the role of his hero, Claudio Malebranche, or "The Falcon," fifteenth-century duke of Ruffano. Duke Claudio is remembered as a madman and a tyrant, but for Aldo, he was a superior being. Believing himself to be a god, Claudio flew over Ruffano. Aldo describes his flight ecstatically: "His arms were wings, he had become a bird. He soared over the rooftops and the city that was his, and the people stared at him in wonder. . . . he was a falcon, and he flew." But of course, as Beo knows, "He was a man and fell. He fell and died" (p. 19). At the end of the novel, Aldo duplicates the Duke's flight and falls to his death.

When I first read *Flight of the Falcon*, the tidy resolution that followed Aldo's fall jarred me out of the story. Responsible Beo dutifully becomes Aldo's heir. Like Duke Claudio's own brother, Carlo the Good, Beo will unite the feuding students and the divided city. He will also complete his brother's backward journey through family and national history, which in retrospect is not mad but unambiguously admirable. The novel ends on an uncharacteristically meliorative note, as if, in *The Scapegoat*, Jean de Gué had renounced his family to his temperate double, John, instead of returning to claim possession. Was du Maurier, always so aware of the perils of inheritance, going soft?

Biography solves the mystery of du Maurier's fall into uplift. The end of *The Flight of the Falcon* is a pious mess because du Maurier herself collaborated with a pious audience. British readers hadn't known what to make of the original novel's violent irresolution. When *Good Housekeeping*, a leading magazine in the America she despised, offered $100,000 for the serial rights on condition that she make the ending more clearly inspirational, she uncomplainingly obliged, despite the dismay of Gollancz, her British publisher, who retained the original ending in the British edition (Forster, p. 337).

In England, Aldo streaks to his death and the novel ends; there follows only a respectful obituary by Ruffano's unworldly Rector, whom Aldo had cuckolded. For America du Maurier added a healing final chapter in which the survivors gather around Beo, who announces his civic mission: "I'll stay with you here in Ruffano. . . . I'll help in whatever way I can. Now that the Rector is back again, he can advise us. First and foremost, I believe Aldo would wish us to continue his work among the poorer students, amongst orphans like yourselves" (p. 250).

In the original novel, Aldo is a satanic and tenacious character who never abdicates on behalf of his tamer brother. He cares not at all about his survivors but only about demonstrating his superhumanity by his glorious and mad flight. Beo, moreover, makes no pledges. Though Aldo does bequeath everything to him, and the Rector's obituary hopes he will "remain with us to carry on the work with orphaned students" (p. 253), after Aldo's fall, Beo himself is silent. The death of his brother is the loss of his narrative voice.

In the novel Daphne du Maurier first wrote, life after Aldo is unformed. Since du Maurier had only mordant suspicion of duty, nobility, and progress, I cannot imagine her writing a character who would grow into his legacy. As I imagine Beo, I assume that beneath his silence, neither can he disentangle himself from the spell of his commanding brother, his family, or his country, nor can he become what they demand: all of Daphne du Maurier's protagonists are maddened by the mentor who embodies the animate past. I assume, too, that despite the rector's faith, Ruffano is not healed by Aldo's suicide. Death pervades du Maurier's novels, but it is never an effective cleanser.

Why did Daphne du Maurier so readily falsify her novel for the American market? Apart from the lure of fat serial rights to an aging writer whose royalties were dropping off and whose glamorously extravagant father had scrounged for money in his last years, she may have found the original *Flight of the Falcon* too flimsy a mask for her own fictional mission: to absorb without being obliterated by the great men whose history incarnated her family and the England in which she had never quite belonged. Had Beo been absorbed into his legacy, Daphne du Maurier might never have emerged to write her final, and finest, novel of male collaboration and dissolution, one set in a vanishing English landscape: the brilliant *House on the Strand*.

The House on the Strand is not a house. Du Maurier claimed that the novel was a history of Kilmarth, her last home, as *The King's General* had been a history of the beloved Menabilly where she had lived for twenty-six years, but Kilmarth, present or past, is not the house of the title, which exists uncertainly somewhere beneath the countryside: "Today, without vertigo or nausea, I could see more clearly that these knolls were not the natural formation of uneven ground, but must have been walls that had been covered for centuries by vegetation, and the hollows, which I had thought, in my dizziness, to be pits were simply the enclosures that long ago had been rooms within a house."[24] A narrator who can scarcely stand, much less see, imagines an irretrievable house buried in an unsteady landscape. The nonexistent house on the possible strand epitomizes the last, lurching journey of Daphne du Maurier's men into each other and abyss.

As her medium of communion, du Maurier borrows from Robert Louis Stevenson's *Strange Case of Dr. Jekyll and Mr. Hyde* the device of a transforming potion, but Stevenson's Victorian gimmick mutates seamlessly into the 1960s, where it becomes a sinister variant of LSD. Moreover, it releases no Mr. Hyde; Dick Young's identity is amorphous but inescapable. The drug is a medium of time travel, but it doesn't transport the body like H. G. Wells's time machine; it liberates the ancestral component of the brain. The scientist Magnus dissects its release of a hidden level of the brain that consists of "our hereditary make-up, the legacy of parents, grandparents, remoter ancestors back to primeval times" (p. 212). This "hitherto untapped ancestral brain" releases in Dick's own metabolism the ancestors who possess Daphne du Maurier's male-centered novels. The legacy has moved inside, where it can devour more efficiently.

Dick's story is not a progress like Julius's; it is a series of trips into a thirteenth century that is always alien and, increasingly, brutal and decimated. Though Dick might have released his ancestral brain, he is no Peter Ibbetson, traveling to his origin: the characters he encounters are implacably distinct from him—"I had not been moving amongst childhood ghosts. The people I had seen were not shadows from my own past. Roger the steward was not my alter-ego, nor Isolda a dream-fantasy, a might-have-been" (p. 86)—and there is no climax of mutual recognition.

Like all fictional time travelers, Dick does find a plot in the past (there is an aborted revolution; he falls in love with Isolda, an oppressed wife who, in another aborted revolution, flees her vicious husband under the protection of her steward, Roger, after her lover is murdered) but he cannot participate in or control that plot: he can only watch and, like a lonely man at the movies, pretend he belongs on the screen.

His final trip takes him to an England wasted under the Black Plague, in which everyone he imagines he knows is slaughtered. This past is no embracing escape; it is an analogue of contemporary devastation: "This was not the world I knew, the world I had come to love and long for because of its magic quality of love and hate, its separation from a drab monotony; this was a place resembling, in its barren desolation, all the most hideous features of a twentieth-century landscape after disaster, suggesting a total abandonment of hope, the aftertaste of atomic doom" (p. 308).

This fragmentary and brutal past is the only England to which Dick has access: in his waking life, Vita, his energetic American wife, is trying to persuade him to move to the United States, or at least to travel with the family to Ireland. Dick wants only to stay in Cornwall, burrowing into the landscape that covers the past. Addicted, infantile, as impotently immature as his name implies, Dick Young is the book's only surviving Englishman. At the end, he lives in the probable paralysis that is one effect of the drug, deserted by his guides but clinging to his land.

An equivocal professor named Magnus first gives Dick the drug and guides him on his trips. This brilliant, presumably homosexual boyhood friend, the enemy of Vita and family life, assumes the role of the powerful, woman-abolishing patriarchs in the earlier books—Paul Lévy, Ambrose Ashley, Patrick Brontë, Jean de Gué, Aldo Donati—but Magnus is an attenuated magus. We hear about their childhood intimacy, but in the novel itself, Magnus appears only as a writer of cryptic letters and a voice on the telephone, continually hanging up and dashing off. His instructions suggest that he knows less about the drug than Dick does (increasingly, he asks questions rather than giving answers), but about two-thirds of the way through, just as he is about to come to Kilmarth and assume his role as guide, he dies violently while on a trip into the past, leaving Dick to plunge on alone.

Magnus is a tantalizing nonpresence who finally evaporates, but Dick has a thirteenth-century guide as well: the good steward Roger, whose track he must follow in his visits. Since Roger lives at Kylmerth, the thirteenth-century Kilmarth, and since he too is in love with the unattainable Isolda, Dick feels that they are merging after the death of Magnus. But Roger, too, leads him only to death.

During the plague, Dick hovers over Roger's deathbed, where he learns that Roger too is a woman-killer—he murdered their beloved Isolda gently, with drugs, to save her from pain and persecution—and a conjurer of spirits. These sudden revelations suggest that Roger conjured Dick, a lapsed Catholic, to grant him absolution on his deathbed. Dick does ironically absolve his supposed master. He then disappears from the past, having lost another guide who, like Magnus, was no guide at all.

Roger killed Isolda, but Dick did not collaborate in the death as Julius Lévy did in his mother's murder or Ambrose Ashley in Rachel's: whether she is alive or dead, it is impossible for him to touch Isolda. In this final, fractured version of du Maurier's male-centered plot, there is no sole murder of a woman to focus the action. In this novel, women are murdered interchangeably in the present and the past.

Isolda is murdered only retrospectively and offstage, but her death is paralleled in the present when Dick begins to strangle his wife Vita: in a dislocating episode when the past invades Kilmarth without the spur of the drug and the house exists on two planes simultaneously, Vita blends with the thirteenth-century villain Joanna and Dick begins to kill her. Just as neither Magnus nor Roger crystallizes as guide, this climactic woman-murder doesn't happen, but though women scarcely figure in *The House on the Strand*, they are in constant danger. There is a sadistic, narratively gratuitous sequence in which a medieval widow is publicly debased for supposed carnality; Isolda is controlled entirely by her coarse husband, then by chivalrous Roger. In the thirteenth century and the twentieth, life is bleak and dangerous for women who live by men's rules of marriage and barter.

In *The House on the Strand*, du Maurier's old male-centered plot decomposes and no new one rises in its place. Men who cannot quite penetrate each other collaborate in murders that never quite happen, yet the women in this novel live under sentence of murder all the time.

The House on the Strand is a book without moorings. Even the land is unsteady, for there are houses underneath with lost worlds in them; moreover, as Dick learns on his trips, rugged Cornwall was once under water. The same underwater instability decomposes du Maurier's patriarchal plot. If Dick Young embodies England, as Philip Ashley did, he is an immobilized citizen of a drowned world.

Daphne du Maurier's male-centered plot was always a story of decomposition. If, as I think, that plot began as a coded chronicle of her grandfather and father, suffusing each other's consciousness, becoming each other's mediums for art, abortive rebellion, and the murder of women, that story devours itself in *The House on the Strand*. It is not exorcised, any more than the past is for Dick, but like the houses beneath the land and the water that once covered it, this lethal collaboration is a perpetual presence. Its reiterated story is so vivid and compelling that we turn to romances like *Rebecca* with relief because they do not force us to become woman-killing men; they only compel us to live with such men.

5

Rebecca and Romance

Here, at last, is the *Rebecca* chapter. It makes me nervous to begin, not because I don't enjoy reading and writing about *Rebecca*, but because I'm imagining a reader who reads *only* this chapter, skipping my impassioned re-creations of out-of-print novels she never heard of. In very bad moments, I imagine a reader thumbing through this chapter in a bookstore and putting down my book because I sound too sardonic—or because I treat *Rebecca*, not as the climax of Daphne du Maurier's achievement, but as an experimental byway in a long career devoted to the study and the creation of powerful men. If this happens, even though I've withheld her until almost the end, Rebecca will have triumphed in my book as she does in her own, overshadowing and weighing down the living.

Few readers remember Daphne du Maurier's men, but everyone remembers her women's men. Hulking, boasting, presiding, the moody males in her three best-known so-called romances—*Jamaica Inn*, *Rebecca*, and *Frenchman's Creek*—overwhelm their female prey, but they have no stories of their own. These impenetrable creatures exist to master women. They strut about and own things, but unlike the haunted heroes we have just left, they are not alive on their own terms.

For me, there is something embarrassing—or "wain" in the du Mauriers' code—about these three women-centered romances. They have kept Daphne du Maurier's name alive, but at the cost of her imaginative audacity. The trapped women through whom we experience the action are all immobilized: Mary Yellan in *Jamaica Inn* is supposed to be spunky, but the plot makes her prey to a series of abducting men, all more or less rapacious and insane; most are bad, one is mad, and the last one, who may be both, winds up as her lover. In *Frenchman's Creek*, Lady Dona St. Columb is as spunky and as helpless as Mary Yellan. Oscillating between two men she belongs to—her dreary husband and "the Frenchman," her imperious pirate lover—she is driven to return to a third needy male, her adored son, after an ecstatic interlude on the pirate ship. The Frenchman seals her fate in an aphorism that governs all three romances: "there is no escape for a woman."[1] There is certainly none for the wife who tells the story of *Rebecca*. Throughout the novel she is a docile companion to the overbearing rich—first to a dreadful American, Mrs. Van Hopper, and then, as wife, to the beautifully mannered landowner Maxim de Winter—with no control over the plot in which Maxim presides and falls.

These brutal tales are not, in the common sense, romances. Technically, they are scarcely romances at all if, as its most articulate readers claim, romances seduce their female readers into "good feelings" about the dominion of men and the primacy of marriage.[2] Romances, like everything we read, move through pockets of tension and subversion, but romance is inherently a soothing and tender genre that aims to reconcile women to traditional lives whose common denominator is home.[3]

Daphne du Maurier's woman-centered novels are scarcely soothing, and none lets its heroine rest in a traditional home. *Jamaica Inn* ends with its heroine a vagabond; in *Frenchman's Creek*, Lady Dona's return home is a bitter if inevitable defeat; home in *Rebecca* is an *unheimlich* monstrosity whose only alternative is exile. If Daphne du Maurier writes romances at all, their achievement is to infuse with menace the lives women are supposed to want.[4] If, as most people think, she is exclusively a writer for women, she glorifies, not the lives to which we are supposed to resign ourselves, but our insatiable desire to be somebody else, somewhere else.

Never do these works bring a willing woman reader to the home where she belongs, nor do they lure her into love. Only one of the three heroines marries the man she loves, and for her, wifehood is an excruciating ordeal with or without a homicidal husband. In all three novels, menaced and solitary women are the quarry of gargantuan enigmas called men. Their stories are less about love than about brow-beating and submission. All abandon the psychic complexity of the male-centered novels; in all, the men have no interiority and the women have no alternatives. I find it odd and ironic that such brutal depictions of emptiness should be given the label "romance."

"There is no escape for a woman." Of course, we no longer believe that. We are free, at least free enough to condescend to sixty-year-old popular novels. We can discount Daphne du Maurier: she wrote lu-gubrious pieties for conventional readers in the post- and prefeminist 1930s; she wrote about the privileged families she lived in, in which men cavorted and displayed themselves while women clucked; she was so male-identified that she consigned women to dreary lives with-out a twinge of empathy. Yesterday's dream is easily diagnosed and dismissed, but superior as we are, Daphne du Maurier's supposedly romantic novels are alive today, while her more brilliant works have died.

Her most prominent American obituary led off by identifying her as "the author of *Rebecca* and other highly popular Gothic and ro-mantic novels."[5] It went on to quote at length the opening of *Rebecca*, proceeded to summarize *Rebecca*'s plot, then quoted its reviews and du Maurier's own perplexed analysis of its popularity. Finally, the obituary listed the films based on du Maurier's fiction and named some of the biographies and plays she wrote, ignoring the rest of her fiction, including, of course, the male-centered novels I have written about in detail—novels so powerful and complex that they drew me to her over the years and inspired me to write this book.

Why do *Rebecca* and romance continue to define Daphne du Maurier's reputation?[6] *The Scapegoat* and *The House on the Strand* are forgotten; *Jamaica Inn* and *Rebecca* live with us still. Partly, I think, this is because we are lazy: not only journalists who write obituaries, but also literary critics, academic and popular, have gotten sluggish over the years. We like stereotypes because we don't have to think about them: to read something is to dispose of it. We define du Maurier loosely as a romance writer because we have a readymade boilerplate for romances, and so we reduce her to her most dismissible achievement. Her bolder works, the male-centered novels and the tales—works closest to her self-awareness, her family legacy, her vision of psychic oppression and doom—are ignored, I think, because they disturb our critical need for the simple-minded and the silly. The rampant definition of Daphne du Maurier as "the author of *Rebecca* and other highly popular Gothic and romantic novels" puts in her place a novelist who, throughout her long career, took artistic risks she hoped would free her from condescending categories.

I fear I sound stuffy. The romances live on because they are fun, and better than fun. *Frenchman's Creek*, the flimsiest and most escapist—and the novel du Maurier herself was most embarrassed by—is unconvincing as a love story and an adventure tale, but as an interweaving of reverie and reality, of the expansive dream-self and the coerced waking role player, it is wonderful in the way *Peter Ibbetson* and *Peter Pan* are wonderful: like them, *Frenchman's Creek* is a dream-vision that deplores ordinary, arid life.

Jamaica Inn is authentically grotesque and weird, and *Rebecca*, of course, is indelible, especially, I think, as a study of menacing domesticity: when the murder plot abruptly begins, about two-thirds of the way through, thus explaining the impalpable oppression of Manderley by a single revelation, the novel thins out into plot-bound suspense. Still, I, like most readers, will never forget the creeping wife in the hating house.

I don't mean to diminish the romances that have become the heart of Daphne du Maurier's reputation, but they do, as I said, embarrass me. I wince at traditional femininity, in and out of books, and so did Daphne du Maurier: if something about the romances makes me cringe, I may not be alone, for du Maurier's own discomfort seems to seep through her luscious prose. I like surprises in my life, in my friends, and in the narrators of novels I read. I gravitate to evasion of categories and, in fiction and life, escape from plot conventions. So did the other Daphne du Maurier, the one who wrote *The House on the Strand*, but in the three romances (especially, of course, *Rebecca*, the only one of the three with a female narrator), the women see only what women are supposed to see: enormous, inescapable men.

These are not soppy women. Mary Yellan is a brave adventurer; Lady Dona St. Columb hates her husband with startling vigor, yearning for erotic transfiguration; the narrator in *Rebecca* is, in her mordant perspective, at least as ghoulish as Mrs. Danvers. But all succumb to this piratical axiom: "There is no escape for a woman." In her imagination, at least, the escape artist Daphne du Maurier refused to remain a woman, but in her romances, she sealed women's escape hatch—though these romances are regularly called "escapist"!

I am uncomfortable with these romances, not only because they are grim—George Eliot's *Middlemarch* is grim, and for that reason critics have always thought it wise—but also because the romances mask themselves as love stories. Love and Daphne du Maurier do not mix well. At thirteen, she wrote crankily to her governess that she had nothing to read but a "soppy book" full of "romantic slush" (Forster, p. 16). She would hate her own romances to be similarly scorned by restless adolescents. She tried to add some acid to the slush, but she didn't de-slush her work altogether.

Frenchman's Creek, that visionary evocation of new horizons, stunts itself with steamy prose: "she was filled with a great triumph and a sudden ecstasy, for she knew then that he was hers, and she loved him, and that it was something she had known from the very beginning . . . she had known then that this thing was to happen, that nothing could prevent it; she was part of his body and part of his mind, they belonged to each other, both wanderers, both fugitives, cast in the same mould" (p. 106). The wanderers and fugitives are the dream protagonists that all three du Mauriers shared, but the heavy-breathing love is Daphne's own female impersonation. The authentic du Maurier world is full of yearning, but there is no love in it.

In *Gerald: A Portrait*, a book whose every word rings true, Daphne collaborated with her lost father, and through him with her mythic grandfather. There, she wrote tartly and startlingly: "But no true harmony can exist between a man and a woman. They rub on each other's nerves. They do not work in tune."[7] The du Maurier men would have secretly agreed, though they would have put it more euphemistically. George du Maurier's novels yearn back toward a lost male fellowship, jolly and tender, for which love between man and woman is a thwarting and inadequate substitute. Onstage, Gerald du Maurier made love by cuffing his women and insulting them; his true communion, in signature roles like Raffles, Arsène Lupin, and Mr. Darling/Captain Hook, was with his own hidden criminal self. As their female heir, Daphne du Maurier felt compelled to write love stories; love was, after all, women's primary talent and business; but she is no more at ease as a lover than Captain Hook would have been.

Jamaica Inn is a savage book; as in the love scenes that were Gerald's specialty, Mary Yellan is repeatedly brutalized by a series of criminal men. There is something erotic about these bullies, but to me, at least, the climactic love story is more disturbing than the villains' abuse. Mary's acceptance of love is a declaration of defeat. Near the end of the novel, she realizes that a woman is, by definition, broken: "She had no will of her own; they could make decisions for her. . . . Once more she knew the humility of being born a woman, when the breaking down of strength and spirit was taken as natural and unquestioned."[8]

When she gets in a rickety cart with Jem—a younger and possibly less mad variant of the other men—she begins a life of unease: "If you come with me it will be a hard life, and a wild at times, Mary, with no biding anywhere, and little rest and comfort. Men are ill companions when the mood takes them, and I, God knows, the worst of them." But by now, she has nowhere else to go. She gets into Jem's cart, she claims, "[b]ecause I want to; because I must; because now and for ever this is where I belong to be" (p. 308).

Jem's undercurrent of menace is close to Gerald's onstage sexiness, and I'm afraid it doesn't turn me on. I live, I know, in more squeamish times than the 1930s; as I write in the late 1990s, the words "abuse" and "battery" are more common in our romantic discourse than "love" or even "sexy"; but I suspect that for Daphne du Maurier, too, the love ending of *Jamaica Inn* was an awkward attempt at feminine affirmation, one that carries less conviction than the novel's assaults.

Rebecca, too, clothes itself as a love story, though elegant Maxim de Winter is only more suavely brutal than her earlier men. Jem offers himself with an affectionate threat: "Men are ill companions when the mood takes them, and I, God knows, the worst of them." Maxim proposes with a similar threat, but in the cultivated language of capitalism. He invites the narrator, not to get on his cart, but to come to Manderley. Since his wife-to-be is a paid companion to the American vulgarian Mrs. Van Hopper, she has as little choice as Mary Yellan when Maxim offers her more of the same: "instead of being companion to Mrs. Van Hopper you become mine, and your duties will be almost exactly the same. I also like new library books, and flowers in the drawing-room, and bezique after dinner. And someone to pour out my tea."[9] Maxim's urbanity is prophetic. Creeping around Manderley in the shadow of its past and the servants who perpetuate that past, she becomes, as Maxim scathingly says, like a "between-maid" who doesn't know her duties. She ends as she began, escorting Max to oppressively sunny watering places, soothing him out of his tyrannical moods as she had Mrs. Van Hopper.

Du Maurier claimed to be astonished when readers equated *Rebecca* with romance. According to her biographer, she read her own novel with harsh acuity:

> She herself saw it as "rather grim," even "unpleasant," a study in jealousy with nothing of the "exquisite love-story" her publisher [and generations of readers] claimed it to be. There was more hatred in it than love, in her own opinion, and she had tried very hard to show her unnamed heroine as intimidated, humiliated and even abused throughout most of the story....she was trying to explore the relationship between a man who was powerful and a woman who was not, just as she had done, in a different way, in *Jamaica Inn* and, to some extent, in everything she had written. She had wanted to write about the balance of power in marriage and not about love. (Forster, pp. 137-38)

This sardonic reader of her most famous romance is the Daphne du Maurier I love. Alas, the *Rebecca* she critiques is not quite the *Rebecca* she wrote. Everything she says about its essential lovelessness is there if we look; even at the end, when the narrator at last inherits the title "Mrs. De Winter," she writes about her achieved marriage in the language of power, not romance: "I suppose it is his dependence on me that has made me bold at last" (p. 9). *Rebecca* has no epithalamium like Jane Eyre's rhapsody: "I have now been married ten years. I know what it is to live entirely for and with what I love best on earth. I hold myself supremely blest—blest beyond what language can express; because I am my husband's life as fully as he is mine."[10]

Still, if *Rebecca* has nothing of what Charlotte Brontë would call love, it exudes worship. In incessant rituals, like an acolyte before an icon, the narrator studies her husband's beautiful, remote, inexpressive face for some sign of how she is supposed to behave. When she learns that Maxim has killed his first wife, she responds with unreflecting empathy, becoming the ideal undiscriminating reader:

> I had listened to his story and part of me went with him like a shadow in his tracks. I too had killed Rebecca, I too had sunk

the boat there in the bay. I had listened beside him to the wind and water. I had waited for Mrs. Danvers' knocking on the door. All this I had suffered with him, all this and more besides. But the rest of me sat there on the carpet, unmoved and detached, thinking and caring for one thing only, repeating a phrase over and over again. "He did not love Rebecca, he did not love Rebecca." (p. 284)

In male-centered novels like *The Progress of Julius*, *My Cousin Rachel*, or *The Flight of the Falcon*, murdering a woman is morally fraught, if not quite a sin. In *Rebecca*, wife-murder sinks to the level of an exciting story because the stupefied narrator makes it one. Her rapt attentiveness to Maxim may not be quite love as Daphne du Maurier or Charlotte Brontë or I would define it, but it does distract us from considering the power dynamic that du Maurier claimed was the novel's subject. Maxim is not, as the narrative presents him, a master or a man; he is an inscrutable, ever-fascinating work of art.

Daphne du Maurier was a better feminist critic of her romances than she was a romance writer. *Frenchman's Creek*, *Jamaica Inn*, and *Rebecca* may not be love stories, but they look and feel like love stories: because they are about women, du Maurier subdues the ruthlessness dominant in her male-centered novels and her tales. I'm sure, despite her disclaimers, that du Maurier had an eye on the market when she simulated love in her three romances. Like that of her grandfather and father, her art was synonymous with audience pleasing, but unlike them she was a woman, so despite her instincts, she wrote, in her woman-centered works, palpitating prose. If women want readers, women must make love.

This enforced love is what embarrasses me about du Maurier's romances: I hate to see women, especially women as bold and gifted as Daphne du Maurier, simulating emotion in prostitute-like fashion. (Of course, men too simulate love, but for their chosen purposes, not to reassure captious spectators.) I am particularly distressed because du Maurier was an incisive, if not entirely forthright, reader of gender regulations in her day (regulations that still cling to our own time): she saw that ruthlessness and pathology belong in male-centered novels, while love, or its simulation, must be attached to women.

I know well this mandate to love. Like du Maurier, I am appalled at the ease with which people I don't know very well assume I love them; they imagine they know what I'm feeling because I'm a woman and I smile; but unlike du Maurier, I am clumsy at the idioms and deceits of romance, so instead of writing a masked novel like *Rebecca*, I smile in public and growl in private.

Cannily, du Maurier made her women-centered novels look like love stories, but all withhold emotion, focusing instead on dynamic isolation. Even the narrator of *Rebecca* shakes off her scrutiny of Maxim when offered the luxury of solitude: "Maxim was in London. How lovely it was to be alone again. No, I did not mean that. It was disloyal, wicked. It was not what I meant. Maxim was my life and my world" (p. 151). In *Rebecca,* as in most women's fiction (and lives), solitude is a fitful blessing and a necessary respite from the need to pump up love where none exists.

Du Maurier's women manage to sound like lovers, but they are, I fear, closer to women's own sense of ourselves in the present day: they are sites of disease. The overwrought idiom of love that masks women's innate decay makes these three novels particularly unsettling in our disease-obsessed age. For du Maurier, to be a man is to be mad, or something close to it, but to be a woman is to be rotten or, at best, defective. Honor Harris, the crippled narrator of *The King's General,* defines herself on behalf of all of du Maurier's female perceivers: "It was thus, then, that I, Honor Harris of Lanrest, became a cripple, losing all power in my legs from that day forward until this day on which I write, so that for some twenty-five years now I have been upon my back, or upright in a chair, never walking any more, or feeling the ground beneath my feet."[11] Like Honor, like Mary Yellan after she learns that "she had no will of her own; they could make decisions for her," du Maurier's female storytellers watch, immobilized, moved from place to place by others as men plunder, boast, and kill.

Du Maurier's most independent women are not always paralyzed;

more often, they are devoured from within, usually by some variety of female cancer. We all remember Rebecca's posthumously diagnosed uterine cancer, along with the "malformation of the uterus" her doctor throws in for good measure, though "it had nothing to do with the disease" (p. 367). On the surface, these ailments are there to exculpate Maxim—since Rebecca was dying, she goaded him to kill her, and thus the murder becomes a kind of suicide—but they also stigmatize a woman "rotten" in her stubborn self-sustainment (like Daphne du Maurier herself, Rebecca has a passion for sailing and extramarital sex), a woman who, according to choric Mrs. Danvers, laughs at men instead of loving them. As Maxim sputters in one of his less debonair locutions, "She was not even normal" (p. 271).

The perverse Rebecca-worship of sinister Mrs. Danvers, and the obscene growths and swollen sea that threaten to devour Manderley throughout the book, might define Rebecca as a lesbian, but nothing in the plot supports this: her great trespass is not loving women but laughing at men. As a woman without love but a consummate simulator of love, Rebecca is, as Maxim claims, "rotten through and through," and thus she deserves to be killed from without and within. Maxim's account of Rebecca's death is full of moral bluster. The slimy Julius Lévy in du Maurier's earlier, forgotten *Progress of Julius* defined more acutely why certain women should die: "It served Mère right. She deserved to die after going with Jacques Tripet. He could understand why Père had killed her. He didn't want his thing to be spoilt. He would not allow anyone else to have it."[12]

Throughout Daphne du Maurier's fiction, uterine cancer is a recurrent symptom, not of lesbianism, but of the refusal to love. The betraying mother in *The Flight of the Falcon* dies of "cancer of the womb." In *The Parasites*, a more complicated mother—a great dancer more at home alone than with her family—is eaten by what we assume is uterine cancer, or, as she puts it, "There's something gone wrong inside."[13] Like Rebecca, she commits semi-suicide rather than losing self-control, but unlike Rebecca, she is eloquent about the disease that is womanhood: "It's queer how a woman is made....There is something deep inside that can't be explained. Doctors think they know all about it, but they don't really. It's the thing that gives life—whether it's dancing, or making love, or having babies—it's the same as the creative force in a man, but men have it always. It can't be destroyed. With us, it's different. It lasts only a little while, then goes. It flickers, and dies, and you can't do anything about it. You have to watch it go. And once it's gone there's nothing left. Nothing at all ... " (p. 70).

Rebecca's uterine problems can be read as a crude punishment for adultery, but if we read nothing but *Rebecca*, we oversimplify Daphne du Maurier's hopeless view of the female condition. Always, for good women and bad, "there's something gone wrong inside." Uterine cancer may punish the dancing mother in *The Parasites* for her emotional elusiveness, but at the end of the novel her dutiful daughter Celia, an avid family caretaker, develops fibroid tumors; despite her yearning for children, she is doomed to a hysterectomy.[14] Crippled or cancerous, du Maurier's women are doomed, not because they are weak—almost always, they are saner and more self-sufficient than her men—but because they are not really women. Like du Maurier herself, they do not love enough, or well enough, or consistently enough, or at all. Within the novels, bodies crumble or eat themselves, but the novels themselves—at least the three famous romances—are stricken with a different, more elusive symptom: a pervading discomfort with the attitudes of love, a discomfort that embarrasses the reader no matter how enthralled she is. Du Maurier's ultimate punishment was not uterine cancer, which never touched her, but the fact that these embarrassed novels now stand for the writer she was.

The debility that devours du Maurier's women is one of many distinctions between her novels and those of Charlotte and Emily Brontë. Comparison with the Brontë sisters clings to her romances as tenaciously as cancer clings to the wombs of her rebellious women, but du Maurier's woman-centered novels have none of the progressive fervor of *Wuthering Heights* or *Jane Eyre*.

It is easy to assume that simply because they were women, Charlotte and Emily Brontë would inspire a later woman who wrote about moors, though the Cornish and the Yorkshire moors are not the same. For Avril Horner and Sue Zlosnik, "the choice of the Brontës as literary forebears may be seen as part of a search for a female writing identity."[15] Alison Light is more expansive in her assumption of female liberation via the Brontës: "The heaviest of du Maurier's debts to the Brontës was to a romantic tradition which centered on feeling and which claimed the importance of romantic love as a potentially dangerous place where the individual, and especially the woman, might get taken 'beyond herself,' uncover hidden desires and often destructive wants. Du Maurier put romance back into the landscape of individualism; her love-stories are also *Bildungsromane*."[16]

But these exegeses of Daphne du Maurier, Romance Writer, refrain from cutting to her romances' cold heart: du Maurier did at times sound like a Brontë, but her heroines scarcely find power and meaning through love. Far from fueling their individualism, romance breaks them down. The Brontës' novels are a surge toward freedom; for du Maurier's women, such elation is too remote to dream about. Moreover, even female Victorian novelists were not likely to have inspired a writer who wrestled so tenaciously with her Victorian patrimony. Daphne du Maurier was never a reverent heir of Victorians, whether male or female. She draws on *Jane Eyre* and *Wuthering Heights* as she does on *Peter Ibbetson, Trilby*, and *Peter Pan*: rather than echoing Victorian sources, she prods and twists their faith in progress and the individual until that faith collapses into her own sense of doom.

Du Maurier adopted *Wuthering Heights* in her first novel, a saga named *The Loving Spirit* after a line in Emily Brontë's poetry. But despite its moors and its wildness, *Wuthering Heights* is a tougher, more triumphant work than any of du Maurier's novels. Its primary narrator, Nelly Dean, is a vigorous, take-charge woman who, though she is a servant, exerts overt and underhanded control over the turbulent action—unlike her ostensible better, the second Mrs. de Winter, who, as *Rebecca*'s narrator, can only stare dreamily at encroaching events.

Emily Brontë's mother-daughter Cathys are brisker, more active women than du Maurier's are allowed to be. Even after her death,

Catherine Earnshaw Linton (Catherine Heathcliff in her heart) plays the role of divine-demonic inspiration to those who follow her. If she resembles any du Maurier woman, it is another overpowering predecessor who survives death to haunt the littler living: Rebecca herself, not *Rebecca*'s timid narrator. Like Rebecca, Catherine marries a great house and endures its stiff, tradition-bound master. Like Rebecca, she gives up her ego to her role.

Unlike Rebecca, though, Catherine has a Heathcliff, who is not only lover and brother but also conscience and shared soul, a towering reminder of the littleness of her marriage. In keeping with the lovelessness of du Maurier's fiction, Rebecca has no Heathcliff, only assorted sexual toys and Favell, her lewd, sponging cousin, who in his parasitic cowardice is certainly no towering conscience. Rebecca de Winter is trapped in the decadent world that Catherine Linton stooped to inhabit.

Moreover, there is nothing malformed or diseased about Catherine's uterus: she dies, not of murder or cancer, but in childbirth, like a proper Victorian woman, giving birth to a daughter who will make the world better. Young Cathy proves to be as take-charge a woman as Nelly Dean, cultivating both her home and her uncouth husband-to-be until they are worthy of her new order. Meantime, her mother energizes the novel by haunting it. Catherine is a far more effective ghost than Rebecca: Rebecca strangles those who come after with her oppressive perfection, while Catherine appears and withholds herself with galvanizing intensity. The posthumous energy that chokes Manderley purges *Wuthering Heights*.

Emily Brontë is an equally uncongenial presence in *The Loving Spirit*, an ambitious family saga based on four generations of Cornish shipbuilders whose history du Maurier studied with the same ardent intelligence she would soon apply to her own family. Janet Coombe, its presiding genius, longs to go to sea but marries her stolid cousin instead. She lives through the generations as the regal figurehead on the family's prize ship. As the *Janet Coombe* deteriorates, the family declines, until, in the 1920s, the fourth generation reverently restores its fortunes.

The novel is a tonal mess; Dickensian melodrama about a wicked capitalist uncle alternates with sardonic domestic satire and Lawrentian spiritual/erotic yearnings, but Janet Coombe's symbolic primacy unifies its disarray. Du Maurier makes Janet a more respectable version of her own great-great-grandmother Mary Anne Clarke, an invisible female force who directs the rivalries and posturing of men. In her first work, du Maurier had not yet found her male voice; her perspective is decorously female. Accordingly, she dubiously rewards Janet's rebelliousness by making her a matriarch. *The Loving Spirit* tries not to ask whether the sea-loving Janet is content to turn into an inspiring figurehead or whether she would prefer to be an inspired sailor like Daphne du Maurier herself—or du Maurier's demonic alter ego, Rebecca de Winter.

The Loving Spirit courts comparison with *Wuthering Heights*. Not only does it take its title from one of Emily Brontë's poems; other Brontë poems begin each of the four sections. But *The Loving Spirit* is a *Wuthering Heights* in which all the ferocious yearning to escape dissipates into a family stronger than any of its members. Early in the novel, Janet prophesies her own immortality: "I'll not bide in Heaven, nor rest here in my grave. My spirit will linger with the ones I love—an' when they're sorrowful I'll come to them; and God Himself won't keep me."[17]

Catherine in *Wuthering Heights* similarly plans to cry in heaven for home, but not out of concern for loved ones: she cares only about what she loves. Her dream, or prophecy, is one of the most powerful egoistic boasts in British literature: "heaven did not seem to be my home; and I broke my heart with weeping to come back to earth; and the angels were so angry that they flung me out, into the middle of the heath on the top of Wuthering Heights, where I woke sobbing for joy."[18]

Janet Coombe's altruism may be more admirable than Catherine's ferocity of desire, but it is also less effective. When, in an eerie reminder of *Peter Ibbetson,* Janet does return from death to comfort her devastated sailor son, she is an ineffectual ghost. Her son Joseph, the most vigorous character in the novel, is no better for his mother's brief visit; he remains blind, maddened, and broken. The ghost of Emily Brontë's Catherine heralded a sphere beyond houses or property; immortality in *The Loving Spirit* is bounded by the family that contains it.

Wuthering Heights, like *The Loving Spirit*, is a saga that produces a saving couple in the young generation, but Emily Brontë's Hareton and young Cathy are a progressive pair: they read and learn, they garden, they sweep away the tangled feuds of the Grange and abandon the Heights to its passionate ghosts. Daphne du Maurier's saving couple, Joe and Jennifer, renew the family by looking backward. These cousins fall in love reading, not improving books, but old family letters. Joe restores the family shipbuilding trade, and Jennifer dispels Janet Coombe's resentful yearnings by announcing complacently: "people can say whatever they damn well please, about work, ambition, art, and beauty—all the funny little things that go to make up life—but nothing, nothing matters in the whole wide world but you and I loving one another, and Bill kicking his legs in the sun in the garden below" (p. 364). The family that in 1830 was too narrow to hold its best members becomes, in 1930, the only sanctuary for the diminished young.

The Loving Spirit is a canny first novel. Its progressive structure masks a bleak sense of a world closing in; its evocation of Emily Brontë (who was not at all a loving spirit) dignifies du Maurier's material, but it obliterates the rage to improve, the faith in the future, that inform *Wuthering Heights* and even such post-Victorian family histories as Galsworthy's *Forsyte Saga*. In *The Loving Spirit*, the future, like Janet Coombe, has nowhere to go.

This dead end characterizes du Maurier's female-centered so-called romances. Superficially Victorian in their idiom, allusions, and sometimes their settings, they have none of the combativeness of actual Victorian novels. Daphne du Maurier raises the ghosts of Charlotte and Emily Brontë to dispel their hopes. *Jamaica Inn*, one of her most popular adventure stories, is set in the nineteenth century. Like many Victorian heroes, Mary Yellan is an orphan. She travels from the cultivated south to live with her aunt in the rugged north. When, in

Elizabeth Gaskell's *North and South* (1855), Margaret Hale makes a similar journey, her honor and courage (and some help from the contriving author) allow her to preside over every environment she enters, but Mary Yellan travels north only to be conquered.

Three ravaging men dominate *Jamaica Inn*: the giant Joss Merlyn, an animalistic caricature of male violence, all drunken threats and broken teeth; his vagabond brother, Jem; and a psychotic albino vicar, who imagines himself a Druid divinity, the spirit of a tor. Mary spends the novel bouncing from one to the other. Her progress is an increasing loss of control. Du Maurier's intense evocation of the Cornish moors is meant to recall *Wuthering Heights,* but Brontë's Catherine belonged on the moors, while Mary is dragged about on them by one or another abductor. Women belong neither in houses nor outdoors. Only du Maurier's giant men are allowed to emanate from the landscape.

A Brontë heroine like young Cathy or Nelly Dean or Jane Eyre would surely tame Jem Merlyn—who orders Mary around and talks gaily about wifebeating—before marrying him, but Mary meekly gets into Jem's cart, not daring to correct him in anything. The Victorian veneer of *Jamaica Inn* is a dismal comment on the progress of romance.

Rebecca evokes Charlotte Brontë's *Jane Eyre* as deliberately as *The Loving Spirit* and *Jamaica Inn* evoked *Wuthering Heights.* As with her earlier novels, du Maurier resuscitates a Brontë sister to dash her hopes. *Jane Eyre* is, like *Rebecca*, a class romance, the first-person narrative of a poor working girl whose moody employer falls in love with her. Like Maxim, Brontë's Rochester is hag-ridden by a first wife, the secret of whose demonic existence he alone knows. Like Maxim's Manderley, Rochester's Thornfield burns down at the end, leaving its owner crippled and diminished, but a husband at last.[19]

Jane Eyre, though, is about a reformer. Jane is a proud, self-affirming narrator; Mrs. de Winter is crushed and humble even when she is a wife. As a pauper, Jane refuses to accept her place; as lady of the manor, the fragile Mrs. de Winter cringes before the servants. Jane combats Rochester's sultanic pride even before she learns of his intended bigamy; Mrs. de Winter stands helplessly by as Maxim verbally cuffs her around, confesses, and falls. Subdued from beginning to end, she does nothing to tame a landowner far more dangerous than Rochester.

The marriage that ends *Jane Eyre* rewards Jane's integrity: only after making her own life and finding her own family does she return to Rochester, no longer a servant but "an independent woman." The marriage that ends *Jane Eyre* begins *Rebecca*, but in Daphne du Maurier's revision, marriage is not an entitlement but a trap. In *Jane Eyre*, a concluding marriage was an emblem of independence. *Rebecca* turns its focus to marriage itself and its stupefying dependence. Mrs. de Winter marries into the life from which Jane Eyre saved herself by asserting herself.[20] A Victorian celebration of autonomy and growth becomes, in the twentieth century, a romance of self-submergence.

Like Rebecca, Maxim's second wife is always about to drown in her role, and so is Manderley itself. The novel begins with a famous dream, in which the narrator envisions herself haunting, as Rebecca did, a Manderley whose drive has "gone native," choked with "name-less parasites" (p. 2). But the Manderley of the nightmare is not far from the Manderley she lived in, whose drive was already overgrown; at the end of "this drive that was no drive," engulfed by giant trees, was the "incredible profusion" of Rebecca's blood-red rhododendrons (pp. 64-65). The Manderley of which the narrator dreams is the same besieged Manderley she knew.

At the end of *Jane Eyre*, though Thornfield has burned, Jane and Rochester move to Ferndean, Rochester's subsidiary estate, where they thrive like the trees that overgrow them. After Manderley burns, the couple has nowhere to go but a succession of alien watering places, where the sun blazes and nothing grows. As the narrator warns at the beginning that is also the end, "There would be no resurrection." *Rebecca* disavows the progress and continuity inherent in even the most subversive Victorian novels. Like Evelyn Waugh's *Handful of Dust* (1934), which had appeared four years earlier, it is a romance about England's last days.

Even in its flourishing time under Rebecca's management, Manderley was no repository of tradition; at its best, it was an empty showplace, menaced by the sea on the west and the overgrowth on the east. Rebecca, not generations of magisterial de Winters, furnished and designed the estate, and hated it as well: a London creature, Rebecca fled Manderley for the city whenever she could. Like a conscientious tour guide for stately homes, Mrs. Danvers reverently preserves the room Rebecca scarcely slept in: her true homes were the cottage by the bay and her London flat. Only Maxim was fatuous enough to believe that Manderley would have an heir, and out of fear that another man had fathered that nonexistent child he killed Rebecca.[21] Before either wife lived in it, Manderley was dead to the future. *Rebecca* is not only Daphne du Maurier's first novel with a female narrator, it is her first work about England's last days. When a woman tells the story, it is always, for du Maurier, a story of loss.

The Brontës, if there ever was such an entity, do inhabit Daphne du Maurier's romances, but in twisted, diminished shape. Their tales of progress and reform, in which purposeful women take control of a future that dissolute men can't control, have no place in du Maurier's choked-off England. Du Maurier draws on Charlotte and Emily Brontë's novels in the same spirit in which she draws on her grandfather's: just as the glorious ancestral reunion of *Peter Ibbetson* becomes, in *The House on the Strand*, a deranged and incoherent possession, so the forward thrust of *Jane Eyre* and *Wuthering Heights* becomes, in du Maurier's so-called romances, a strangled lunge into inescapability. We do Daphne du Maurier a disservice if we gloss her novels by equating her with the Brontës or any other Victorians. Victorian fiction was her inheritance, but her ironic despair, and her compulsive self-masking, make her a writer of the next century who, in the course of her long writing life, obliquely glossed her own most famous work.

Her tales are obscure today; even "Don't Look Now" and "The Birds," the bases of well-known films, are scarcely read, though they are more starkly frightening than the films that live on under their names. Most of the tales are opaque and unresolved crystallizations of the tightly plotted novels, rather than miniature versions of them.

One in particular, "The Blue Lenses," is a distillation of the second wife's story in *Rebecca*, with all trappings of romance stripped away.

"The Blue Lenses" (1959) is an extract of wifeliness as *Rebecca* defines it. *Rebecca* courts ghosts and plays with Brontësque atmosphere, but it stops short of the supernaturalism that "The Blue Lenses" embraces. Convalescing from an eye operation, a once-contented wife sees with washed eyes her nurses, doctors, and husband: all wear the heads of predatory animals. When the lenses are removed, the animal heads disappear. She thinks she is cured of what must have been a hallucination until she sees in the mirror that her own eyes are "doe's eyes, wary before sacrifice, and the timid deer's head was meek, already bowed."[22] The operation has allowed her to see her life too well.

In *Jamaica Inn*, Mary knew the kindly vicar was mad when she found his savage caricatures of his congregation as sheep and himself as a wolf. In popular romantic novels, such a vision must be diagnosed and dismissed, but in the more obscure genre of the tale, it returns. Daphne du Maurier's tales divulge a similar hidden bestiality; they expose the predation within the pieties. The vicious cul-de-sac of "The Blue Lenses" reveals more about *Rebecca* than does the progressive confidence of *Jane Eyre*.

Du Maurier's male-centered novels, now forgotten and out of print, give us a sharply etched, unsentimental version of the story that in *Rebecca* is veiled, obscured, like Manderley, by its surrounding overgrowth. If we read *Rebecca* in isolation from du Maurier's more daring fiction, we can prettify and trivialize it (as do the various film adaptations). But *Rebecca* is easy to diminish and revise, for unlike du Maurier's more vivid and vigorous fiction, it gains intensity from everything we don't know.

Rebecca herself is notoriously obscure. Maxim's moral fulminations tell us little about her; the cold, boyish, sea-loving rebel whom Mrs. Danvers describes sounds less like Maxim's monster than like Lady Dona St. Columb, the romantic heroine of *Frenchman's Creek*—and, of course, like Daphne du Maurier herself. All these wild Rebeccas mesh uneasily with the polished chatelaine who casts so intimidating a shadow at the beginning. Rebecca is a perfect woman in the novel's first half, then, in the second, she turns into a woman who is perfectly evil, because unwomanly. She is less a coherent character than a series of discordant images.

Rebecca has to be cloudy, since she is dead, but her vital interpreter, Mrs. Danvers, is equally undefined. Mrs. Danvers is conventionally played as a sepulchral lesbian, but who, then, was Mr. Danvers? Is "Mrs." a mere courtesy title denoting household authority, as it was for "Mrs." Nelly Dean in *Wuthering Heights*? But *Wuthering Heights* is set in the eighteenth century, when "Mrs." was a common mark of status for a mature woman. By the time *Rebecca* was published, "Mrs." rarely designated female authority. In this book, the title is a token of deprivation and infantilization.

The virtuous narrator herself is as darkly defined as the evil characters. Compared to du Maurier's male protagonists, whose psychic turbulence we share—Julius Lévy in *The Progress of Julius*, Philip Ashley in *My Cousin Rachel*, Dick Young in *The House on the Strand*—she is delicately but firmly sealed from us. It is common to assume that she is too negligible to have a name other than "the second Mrs. de Winter," which she is rarely called, but she does have a "lovely and unusual" name (p. 24) we never learn; she begins to trust Maxim when he spells it correctly. The lovely and unusual name that is hard to spell may be "du Maurier"; it may be "Brontë"; it may be so rare that it is unimaginable. Whether or not we can guess her name, it is veiled from us, as is the childhood, the family history, and the adored father that she describes to Maxim during their first luncheon. The narrator of *Rebecca* appears negligible because she is even more shrouded than Rebecca was. She appears passive because she muffles herself. Such shadowy characters are unusual in Daphne du Maurier's fiction. Her men spring vividly and dimensionally to life, complete with their ancestral pasts, but the second Mrs. de Winter, who secretes from us her lovely, unusual name, blocks our reading of her because she spends most of her story trying vainly to read her still more inscrutable husband.

When she first meets Maxim, they are scarcely soulmates. She sees him as a beautiful anachronism: "He belonged to a walled city of the fifteenth century, a city of narrow, cobbled streets, and thin spires, where the inhabitants wore pointed shoes and worsted hose. His face was arresting, sensitive, medieval in some strange inexplicable way, and I was reminded of a portrait seen in a gallery I had forgotten where, of a certain Gentleman Unknown" (p. 15).

Throughout their marriage, even after his confession, Max remains "a certain Gentleman Unknown" whose beautiful face it is her Psyche-like task to read and interpret. We never know her own face, but we share with her the tiring chore of learning Maxim's and the relief of occasional vacations from it: "If Maxim had been there I should not be lying as I was now, chewing a piece of grass, my eyes shut. I should have been watching him, watching his eyes, his expression. Wondering if he liked it, if he was bored. Wondering what he was thinking. Now I could relax, none of these things mattered" (p. 151). Even at the very end, when all secrets have been revealed and Maxim has trusted her alone with knowledge of his guilt, he is shut to her: "Maxim did not answer. I glanced sideways at his face but it told me nothing" (p. 371).

The supposed domestic intimacy of *Rebecca* involves our identification with a nameless, faceless "I" reading the inscrutable hieroglyph of a blank man. Too many supposedly sophisticated readers have implicated Daphne du Maurier in the wife she impersonates so knowingly. In her witty essay on female Gothic romances, Joanna Russ pinions the omnipotent, unknowable men of du Maurieresque romance under the label "the Super-Male." Russ glosses the compulsive face-reading of Mrs. Super-Male as the busywork necessary for female survival: "When the most important person in your life is your man, when you can't trust him (and can't trust anyone else), it becomes exceedingly important to 'read' other people's faces and feelings. This is what most real women spend their time doing; therefore the novels not only portray them doing it, but glamorize and justify what in real life is usually necessary, but boring."[23]

Russ is a shrewd anatomist of women's lives, but so was Daphne du Maurier. Du Maurier was not, by nature, a romance writer; she knew everything Joanna Russ knows about the mandated lives of shadowed women and the power of illegible men. *Rebecca* is full of obscurity—in its characters as well as its suspense plot—but Daphne du Maurier knows more about men and women and murder than her romances choose to tell. To read *Rebecca* thoroughly, we need to read those seemingly translucent novels in which murderous men tell their own stories. At one point even Maxim hints that he wants to break out of his Super-Male role and participate in the full disclosure of *The Scapegoat* or *Hungry Hill*: "Men are simpler than you imagine, my sweet child" (p. 201), he begins. But his bride remains a sweet child; she asks no leading questions. When Max is finally forced to confess his murder of Rebecca, he does so in the artificial language of melodrama. The novel never lets us live with him.

For Daphne du Maurier too men were simpler than women imagine. She chose to make Maxim de Winter an unknown gentleman because she was writing about a shrouded woman seeing a stylized enigma, but unlike Maxim's nameless second wife, in her clear, strong, male-centered novels, Daphne du Maurier listened to men's stories and she told.

6

Movie Star

As Daphne du Maurier remembered her life, it bristled with possibilities. Protean heir of talent, beauty, and powerful contacts, she could, she claimed, have become either a movie star or a writer. She became a writer, perhaps in partial deference to her cinema-hating father, and perhaps because no director would allow a pretty actress to become man, wife, and boy in turn. After her death, though, she turned into the movie star she remains today.

Movies that live on under the names of her books keep the existence of the writer alive—though not, in most cases, the books. Even the popular *Rebecca* and *Jamaica Inn* are probably less read than refracted through film. As I write my own book, I am confronted with depressingly blank faces when I say (in academics' brutal phrase) that I'm "working on" Daphne du Maurier. These faces then remember Alfred Hitchcock. Yes, they saw his creepy *Rebecca*; yes, his film *The Birds* is a masterpiece of horror. Aficionados remember Nicolas Roeg's luscious Hitchcockian horror film *Don't Look Now* from the 1970s.

Oh, did Daphne du Maurier write the original stories? they say, while their eyes float off into cinematic reveries.

Whether I like it or not, film is remembered because film is the dominant medium of our century. We all think in movie images, not words. Black letters on a white page are obsolete: even our computer screens look more like movie screens than like pages in books. I am writing this on a screen with a color scheme I've designed, a soothing green-on-green, colors I will probably have changed several times by the time I finish this chapter. Even the most colorful prose can no longer compete with the colors that bathe us from screens. No doubt it's sterile and antiquarian of me to lament that Daphne du Maurier's sharp-edged fiction has been softened by the many movies allegedly based on her work. Greater novels than hers, along with innumerable plays and lives, have been swamped and sweetened by their translation to film. Why should this cannily commercial writer be inviolate? Did she want to be?

I am trying to resist my own instinct to see Daphne du Maurier as a victim of a culture eager to patronize women and to dilute what they see and say—though she is that. From a careerist point of view, du Maurier has been lucky to survive at all. She was lucky to inherit her grandfather's artistic adaptability, for George du Maurier too thrived in adaptations: from the beginning his Svengali was indistinguishable from Beerbohm Tree's famous performance, and he lives on today, scarcely on the page, but in actors' fertile imaginings of possessed impresarios. As George's novels courted the theater— particularly through his own stagily posed illustrations of his books —so Daphne's, in their menacing atmosphere, terse dialogue, and whirling plots, have courted the movies.

Daphne du Maurier felt she could be anything: man (mad or sane), woman, wife (good or bad), lady, boy, movie star. Ironically, her versatility strangled her literary reputation, for movies absorbed this uncommon artist into the Daphne du Maurier people giggle at: a genteel romance writer whose throbbing love stories are smothered in atmosphere. But the romance, the love, and the atmosphere all come from the movies. The men who adapted her novels, even the great Alfred Hitchcock, bathed far more cozily in setting and sentiment than she.

Daphne du Maurier survives on film, but at the cost of her defining weirdness. Movies have made her digestible but despised. Alfred Hitchcock's Oscar-winning adaptation of *Rebecca* is, in the eyes of Hitchcock acolyte Robin Wood, tainted by its source: "*Rebecca* (1940) was Hitchcock's first Hollywood film, an expensive production, and one guesses he didn't have much to say on the script. In any case, the film fails either to assimilate or to vomit out the indigestible novelettish ingredients of Daphne du Maurier's book, and it suffers further from Olivier's charmless performance, which finally destroys our sympathy with the heroine, doting on such a boor."[1] The uncharacteristic charmlessness of the great and, in those years, entrancing Laurence Olivier stems, one infers, from the actor's healthily masculine revulsion at an indigestible novel.

Du Maurier's novels have been blamed for everything simpleminded or specious in the films they have inspired, but every film adaptation I have seen has twisted her strange, grim books into the steamy sort of thing a woman named Daphne du Maurier *should* have written: bizarre visions become indigestible novelettish concoctions to which the director can condescend. While most adaptations treat du Maurier's name and material with ostensible reverence, all take away her bite.

The Scapegoat is so fluid and picturesque that it should have made a wonderful movie: the book is a tale of mutual possession, in which a callous, carefree lord of a French manor tricks his inhibited English double into living his life. In this mordant account of family, history, and ownership in a rotting château, we never know where John ends and Jean takes over. John is kind, but without Jean to animate him he would disappear into depressive isolation. By the end of the novel, Jean has appropriated both the dreary routine of John's British life and his borrowed French lordliness. The bereft Englishman has no recourse but to evaporate into a monastery.

Talky and visually constrained, the film *The Scapegoat* (1959;

dir. Robert Hamer) lacks the novel's picturesque descriptions of a corrupted French land and a suavely self-devouring landed class. Alec Guinness plays the double role of John and Jean with dull anguish. No doubt Guinness was expected to reprise his effervescent performance in *Kind Hearts and Coronets* (1949), in which he played all eight members of a lunatic titled family, but in *The Scapegoat* he is muted.

Before he meets his double, du Maurier's John longs to become "the self who clamored for release, the man within" with "a mocking laugh, a casual heart, a swift-roused temper and a ribald tongue."[2] But Guinness's Jean has no laughter, temper, or ribaldry, and his morose John has none to suppress; he casts a lugubrious shadow over both roles. Like other star actors who find themselves in du Maurier movies—Laurence Olivier in *Rebecca*, Richard Burton in *My Cousin Rachel*, Donald Sutherland in *Don't Look Now*— Guinness seems depressed by the material, glimpsing, perhaps, the stinging daughter whose biography exposed the petulant child within her actor-father.

Moreover, the film turns *The Scapegoat* into a morality play du Maurier never wrote, wrenching the novel's fluid relationships into a melodramatic opposition whereby Bad Jean sets up Good John as an alibi so that he, Jean, can murder his wife and run off with his mistress. Good John foils the plot and is rewarded by winning Jean's mistress, who is even more saintly than she is in the novel.

The movie's rigid moral definitions nullify Daphne du Maurier's cool amorality. There is no premeditated murder in her novel; everyone and no one kills Jean's wretched wife, the scapegoat who embodies all the inequities of feudal paternalism, of family hate, of lives without hope, shackled by the past. When Françoise falls out of the window, there is no hint that Jean had secretly returned to push her, but her death does release her miserable family into visions of a renewed future. No one person murdered Françoise, but everyone attached to her profits from her death. Du Maurier's lethal vision of domestic relations is far more comprehensively chilling than the film's re-invention of Jean as a wicked, scheming husband.

In the novel, moreover, Béla, Jean's mistress whom John inherits, is a respite from social viciousness, not a prize. At the end of the novel John may be about to gain his own soul, but no love story is commensurate with his lesson and his loss. The film of *The Scapegoat* is not only duller and more timid than du Maurier's novel; like all the supposedly du Maurieresque films I have seen, it contracts du Maurier's scope, so that her moral skepticism is flattened into poles of virtue and villainy and her cynical anatomies of possession and power sag into love lost or gained.

The Scapegoat is one of the more obscure du Maurier adaptations, but like most others, it is strangely lifeless. A visually scintillating novel becomes a plodding film with more exposition than spectacle. Du Maurier's cinematic novels inspire film makers but then, like the blighting specter of Rebecca, she dampens them as they film on. Perhaps adapters lose heart because the books are refractory: their supposed moral clarity fades into tangles—John and Jean are not so much antagonists as collaborators, presiding jointly over a doomed feudal community—and their supposed romantic appeal is, in essence, a vision of obsession and abuse. *The Scapegoat* is less well known than the others, but it is not the only du Maurier film to turn a novel about hate into a movie about love.

The first adaptation of *My Cousin Rachel* (1952) was splashier than *The Scapegoat*. Richard Burton made his American debut—and received his first Academy Award nomination—playing Philip Ashley to Olivia de Havilland's tactfully inscrutable Rachel. The film is a showpiece for beautiful young Burton, on whose innocence, pain, and despair the camera tenderly dwells. Du Maurier's novel, though, looks *with* Philip rather than at him; like her other male-centered novels, it entices us to enter the sensibility of a woman-killer, one in thrall to an older man—here, his cousin and benefactor, Ambrose, who has married Rachel and died in mysterious terror of her. Ambrose tutors Philip in murderous love. Turning Philip into the misunderstood, love-seeking youth who represented ideal manhood in the 1950s dilutes the evilly alluring world into which Philip's paranoia initiates the reader. Unlike the novel, though, the movie gives us some-one to love.

In the 1980s and 1990s, the BBC serialized a group of Daphne du Maurier novels, including *My Cousin Rachel*, though unsurprisingly, only *Rebecca* was imported to American television. Like all these, *My Cousin Rachel* (1990; dir. Brian Farnham) is a lush production, one whose breathtaking scenery atones for the visual dullness of the black-and-white adaptations of the 1950s. Superficially, it is truer to du Maurier than the 1952 American movie, for it makes Rachel a varied and dimensional character; this time she, not Philip, is the star part. As Geraldine Chaplin plays her, Rachel is angry, volatile, intelligent, and in every way more interesting than the dimpled boy who alter-nately adores her as the ideal woman and hates her as a demon.

As with the old movie, though, we look with some envy *at* the material, and at beautiful Philip within it, rather than sharing the story the inflamed boy constructs. Christopher Guard is a dull actor, but his Philip is softly, sweetly watchable; his pale baby face, bee-stung lower lip, seductive attitudes, beautify Daphne du Maurier's grasping narrator. It is such a pleasure to see Philip seeing that we are protected from the world he sees.

The main activity in this version of *My Cousin Rachel* is not mur-der but horseback riding—in the novel, a logistical necessity, not a spectacle in itself. There are reiterated long sequences of beautiful people on still more beautiful horses galloping for no particular rea-son through woods and voluptuous farmland, along beaches and cliffs: the viewer is less interested in where they are going than she is pos-sessed by a longing to gallop by their side.

Du Maurier's novel is historically sparse; its mystery and rage could erupt in any place and time. By contrast, Hugh Whitemore's BBC adaptation is steeped in Victorian nostalgia. Italy and England are not states of mind but gorgeous rooms in luxuriant villas and estates; the camera pans around them appreciatively for our delectation, not to define the characters who live there. Horses and coaches, fountains and seacoasts, are so lovingly photographed that they overwhelm the human story.

There is a long, feudal Christmas feast with jolly songs, stomping dances, and funny, tipsy peasants. In du Maurier's novel, the Christmas dinner is an unadulterated nightmare; as in similar ceremonies throughout du Maurier's work, the time-hallowed ritual is a mass madness that draws out the madness of the character chosen to preside over it. In this film, the Christmas feast is such jolly fun that Philip's angst is an annoying interruption of our nostalgic delight. Daphne du Maurier's Victorian tale of possession draws us into a poisoned patriarchy. Remade by the BBC, it becomes a paean to lost Victorian deference, to delectable food, to horses, clothes, surfaces, servants. The privilege and power that du Maurier exposes become the sensuous center of our longing, distracting us from the madness at its heart.

When Richard Burton played Philip, he was so beautiful that we were scarcely aware of the dead Ambrose suffusing his mind with terror. The BBC adaptation pays more attention to Ambrose as Philip's master and double, but this Ambrose, like Philip himself, is tender victim rather than murderous agent. The novel begins with the seal of Ambrose and Philip's union: a gibbet on which a wife-murderer swings. Ambrose explains woman-killing to young Philip with his usual urbane misogyny: "It's true his wife was a scold, but that was no excuse to kill her. If we killed women for their tongues all men would be murderers" (p. 10). By the end of the novel, Philip has consummated Ambrose's own wife-murder; he ends contemplating the gibbet and his empty, powerful future as Ambrose's heir.

The BBC adaptation does keep the gibbet, but at several refracted removes and only as a haunting token of guilt: it carries only tangential associations with Ambrose and none with wife-murder. Philip mutters something about Ambrose and the gibbet to Louise, the suitable English girl with whom he fails to fall in love. After Rachel's death, he stands under the gibbet ruminating in voice-over: "They used to hang men. Not any more." Wife-murder is never mentioned.

This gibbet is a symbol of generic guilt, not a particular portent of shared doom. It signifies murder in general, not the woman-murder in which Ambrose and Philip are fated to collaborate.

Du Maurier's men are doomed to kill women; the men in the movie are driven by love to anguished, inadvertent crime. The du Maurier law of sexual antagonism—"no true harmony can exist between a man and a woman. They rub on each other's nerves. They do not work in tune"[3]—mutates, in beautiful BBC England, into a lyrical meditation on lost elegance and impossible adoration.

The BBC *Jamaica Inn* (1985; dir. Lawrence Gordon Clark) is a similarly lingering celebration of England's moors—moors that are primitive and terrifying in the novel. The BBC adaptation is truer to the novel and its setting than is Alfred Hitchcock's bizarre 1939 film, which had no moors at all and only snippets of Daphne du Maurier's plot. Instead, Hitchcock featured interminable shots of angry waves crashing on rocky coasts and an invented villainous squire, Sir Humphrey Pengallan, played by an oozily decadent Charles Laughton who is creepily photographed to resemble Hitchcock himself. Even in this early adaptation, Hitchcock wrestled with du Maurier, doing his best to wrench her obsessions into his own. He strangles her more suavely in his later *Rebecca* and *The Birds*.

Derek Marlowe's BBC screenplay is superficially faithful to the novel. Moors abound, as they do in the book, and the squire who was one of Hitchcock's lurid self-portraits returns to the sidelines where du Maurier had put him. Marlowe restores her clerical villain, the mad vicar Francis Davey, who secretly directs the smugglers while dreaming of himself as the reincarnation of an ancient sun god, the spirit of a tor.

The BBC version seems to restore the novel Hitchcock pillaged, but both adaptations soften du Maurier's brutal love. Both glamorize Mary Yellan, who in the book is a pitiless and increasingly terrified observer of the violence men dole out to each other and to their helpless women. The movie Mary Yellan is like the movie Philip Ashley, no longer a frightful seer, but a pretty actor to be seen. Hitchcock has Maureen O'Hara playing Mary, who is all abundant hair and flouncing gestures and improbably elaborate costumes. Jane Seymour in the BBC version gives the same kind of performance. She has even more hair than Maureen O'Hara, and she wears more makeup; this soignée creature seems like an extraterrestrial dropped in the savage du Maurier landscape of smugglers and moors, abductors and mad gods. Neither actress approximates the clear-seeing, plain-speaking Mary of the novel, who is broken into her surroundings as she learns a woman's lesson: "She had no will of her own; they could make decisions for her….Once more she knew the humility of being born a woman, when the breaking down of strength and spirit was taken as natural and unquestioned."[4] As Maureen O'Hara and Jane Seymour perform this beaten-down girl, being born a woman means waving one's hair around in narcissistic detachment from one's surroundings, surroundings that swallow the girl in the book.

Du Maurier's Mary is terrorized less by smugglers or moors than by her intimates: her aunt Patience, wrecked into a terrified lump by Joss, her sadistic giant of a husband; and Jem, her amorphous love interest. In the novel, Joss and Patience are caricatures of conventional husbands and wives, he all bellowing brutality, she all quivering compliance. As a portent of Mary's own metamorphosis under a man's control, Patience's terror is more frightening than Joss's rages.

In the adaptations, though, Mary has little to fear from her uncle and aunt. Hitchcock's Joss is sometimes irascible, but he's no violent giant; we see more of his obsequiousness to the wicked squire than we do his brutality to his wife. Mary, excluded from most of the action, is grouped with Patience from the beginning; the two of them, equally and decorously feminine, exit and enter at the directive of the men. Patience is no fearful portent of Mary's broken future; they belong together by nature. In the BBC adaptation, Joss (Patrick McGoohan) and Patience (Billie Whitelaw) are a floridly psychotic pair, he tremulous with alcohol and guilt, she simpering about in Ophelia-like garb. McGoohan and Whitelaw are fun, but they are too bizarrely over the top to portend anything about ordinary men, women, or marriage.

Joss's brother, Jem, emanates from du Maurier's smugglers and sadism; when, at the end of the novel, Mary gets into his cart, she may be embracing love, but she may be acquiescing in her aunt's destiny—the only ending her brutal milieu offers. The adaptations struggle to disentangle Jem from his surroundings. Just as Mary becomes a glamorous doll and Joss and Patience are softened into eccentricity, so Jem becomes an alternative to Joss, not Joss's psychosexual kin.

Hitchcock is so ludicrously bent on sanitizing Jem that he makes him, not a smuggler, but a disguised officer of the law. This Jem is so virtuous that he's a fool. When we first meet him, the smugglers are hanging him; fortunately Mary is there to cut him down. Jem repeatedly gives his plans away to the sinister squire. When the squire finally abducts Mary, even doltish Jem realizes his villainy, shoots him, and creeps off furtively with Mary. Superficially, Marlowe's BBC script restores du Maurier's equivocal lover, but Marlowe too goes through purifying gyrations. Though he is no longer an officer of the law, this Jem is, as he keeps insisting, only a horse thief—and he steals only from the pompous squire—not, like his brother Joss, a murderer. He becomes Mary's solicitous guardian, a northern version of Jane Austen's Mr. Knightley, letting her know when she looks well or tired, whether, and where, she should go or stay. He is infallibly right and attractively vulnerable; just as Hitchcock's Jem is almost hanged, Marlowe's Jem is abducted by a group of toughs who are after Mary. Both are more brutalized than brutal. When Mary finally gets in Jem's cart, she does so with a wild grin of erotic abandon; there is no doubt that Jem is the perfect man and destiny is delight. The BBC *Jamaica Inn* may correct the narrative distortions of Hitchcock's movie, but it does so in Hitchcock's spirit, not Daphne du Maurier's. Both soften a grim novel into a romantic movie about love.

Hitchcock's *Rebecca* is the movie everybody knows, but most of us remember it selectively: the movie's wonders are its eccentrics. Mrs. Danvers, the fog, and the malevolent house eclipse the marriage Hitchcock tries to wrench into love.

Alfred Hitchcock purportedly hated Daphne du Maurier's work—throughout the filming of *Rebecca*, he wickedly referred to the browbeaten second wife as "Daphne"—but his du Maurier movies were milestones in his career. *Jamaica Inn* was his last English film, *Rebecca* was his first Hollywood film, and *The Birds*—an open, experimental, unresolved abandonment of well-made storytelling—was his first post-*Psycho* work. Every time Hitchcock turned a corner, Daphne du Maurier helped him around. He grumbled about how hampered he was by her simple-minded femaleness—or, as Robin Wood puts it, "the indigestible novelettish ingredients" of her work—but I suspect that Daphne du Maurier disturbed him because she wasn't novelettish enough. In her books, he found a sensibility even more perverse than his own. In revenge, his three du Maurier films make the novels look sillier and soppier than they are. Those many potential readers who know du Maurier only through Hitchcock's films assume that the soppy parts come from du Maurier, while the sophisticated terror belongs to Hitchcock. So far he has won—unjustly—this battle of images.

Rebecca's opening is swathed in reverence for du Maurier: like all David O. Selznick's productions of the 1940s, it is portentously literary, giving obsequious credit to Daphne du Maurier's "celebrated novel" and beginning in voice-over with Joan Fontaine's insufferably churchy reading of du Maurier's opening paragraph in bowdlerized form. Like the wife in the novel, Fontaine dreams that she went to Manderley again, but she sees no perverse erotic growths there and she omits the uncompromising line, "there will be no resurrection." The opening set piece is made suffocatingly poetic, not menacing and implacable as it is in the novel.

As the opening is swathed in reverence, so the entire movie is swathed in fog. Fog descends on Daphne du Maurier's novel only sparingly, when the plot requires it; for the most part, colors, architecture, rooms, gardens, mannerisms, faces, all are assaultively vivid. Danger lies not in muffled vision but in seeing too much. *Rebecca*'s true fog is within, shrouding motives, not objects: Mrs. de Winter peers at every detail of her husband's face, every turn of his aristo-cratic body, but she cannot penetrate the man within.

In Hitchcock's movie, fog pours all over Manderley most of the time, obliterating the precision of the novelist's scrutiny. Hitchcock's endless disgorgement of fog is a parody of a novel du Maurier never wrote, suggesting that Manderley's domestic mystery is a matter of hokey special effects, not an exposure of power and perversity.[5] Hitchcock's *Rebecca* is smothered in self-conscious atmosphere; du Maurier's is pitilessly clear.

Even more obtrusive than his fog is the romance Hitchcock brings to the de Winters' marriage. In the novel, even before the bride's arrival at Manderley, the marriage is brusque and business-like; Maxim meets Mrs. Van Hopper's gauche young companion, approves her for inscrutable reasons, and offers a barter: "Instead of being com-panion to Mrs. Van Hopper you become mine, and your duties will be almost exactly the same."[6] In the film, there is throbbing atmo-sphere: Joan Fontaine as the girl first meets Olivier's Maxim, not through Mrs. Van Hopper, but as a Byronic figure perched danger-ously on a picturesque cliff. She fears he is about to jump, screams, runs to him, and pulls him back. The implication is that she will save him throughout their marriage (as she does), while the novel implies that the girl will be endlessly taken over and moved about (as she is).

For their wedding, Hitchcock gives the couple an extended pic-turesque ceremony in Italy. The wedding scenes in the movie are so full of cavorting bliss that most viewers would assume that they are straight from gushing du Maurier, but there are no such scenes in the book, whose perfunctory wedding and honeymoon are undrama-tized. The most effective domestic scene in the film, one entirely Hitchcock's, has Maxim at Manderley showing home movies of their blissful Italian honeymoon, while, in the film's present, domestic ten-sions erupt. Big kisses in the sun superimpose themselves over tears in the drawing room.

The scene is a brilliant exhibition of the cruelty of film, but du Maurier's novel imagines no happy past from which the couple falls away: from their first meeting, Maxim is cryptic and imperious, a man we cannot imagine jumping up and down on an Italian beach, much less taking home movies. As far as we see, the marriage was always laced with menace; as du Maurier herself said of *Rebecca*, "There was more hatred in it than love, in her own opinion, and she had tried very hard to show her unnamed heroine as intimidated, humiliated and even abused throughout most of the story."[7]

Hitchcock makes Manderley the problem, not marriage or Maxim, and in Hitchcock's *Rebecca*, Manderley certainly is a problem; it is as hostile to romance as the *Psycho* house will be, and it too is dominated by a stately woman who embodies a fantasy of the past, here not a mummified mother but the sepulchral housekeeper, Mrs. Danvers. Judith Anderson's Mrs. Danvers is so overpowering, Anderson (unlike Olivier) brings such erotic intensity to her scenes with Joan Fontaine, that she makes Olivier's Maxim look normal and breezy, if slight, by comparison.

Far from embodying Manderley, this Maxim de Winter seems hardly more at home there than his new bride is. Du Maurier "had wanted to write about the balance of power in marriage and not about love" (Forster, pp. 137-38), but Hitchcock films an affectionate young couple who make the mistake of wandering into a sinister house, one in the power of a crazy woman, which fortunately burns down at the end. Hitchcock's direction sentimentalizes the material so radically that he hardly needed to soften the novel further by changing its plot.

Hitchcock's Maxim is exonerated of wife-murder: America's Motion Picture Production Code refused to let a hero kill even a promiscuous wife and end the movie unpunished. Moreover, not only Olivier, but also Ronald Colman, who had turned down the part, refused to alienate audiences by killing Rebecca. Thus, Hitchcock's Rebecca falls at the crucial moment and strikes her head on "a heavy piece of ship's tackle" while Maxim stands by, passive and appalled. Moreover, while du Maurier's Rebecca may have goaded Max to murder her in order to avoid a humiliating death by cancer, Hitchcock's Rebecca has definitely done so, as we hear over and over: she is so determined to die, and he is so shrinking, that there is no ambiguity or emotional complexity. Rebecca seems to ask of Max a marital favor he is too inept to fulfill.

Hitchcock suggested that his daring was stymied by the whims of actors and censors, just as he claimed to be hag-ridden by the triviality of Daphne du Maurier herself, but he directs Olivier to give a performance so passive and effete that whatever the script tells him to do, this Maxim seems incapable of killing Rebecca or even of hurting a fly. Olivier's inward-turned portrayal relies on a single gesture: he clutches a head that seems to be falling off. In the big confession scene, in which he blurts out that he hated Rebecca, he puts his hands in his pockets as he reads the line. Through most of the scene, he sits weakly, swathed in an unbuttoned coat that seems too big for him and smoking needily as if the cigarette is a maternal breast. Olivier has been derided for this uncharacteristically limp performance, but Hitchcock surely put the big coat on him and told him to sit during the scene. All power is drained from this Maxim, and so is the impulse to kill.

The end is a triumph of young love, not the stricken exile we see in the novel. In Hitchcock's version, Joan Fontaine does not accompany the men on their odyssey to Rebecca's gynecologist in London;[8] instead, she becomes the focus of the menaced Manderley as mad Mrs. Danvers stalks from room to room with a burning torch, unable, we are told, to bear the thought that Max and his new bride will live happily there. In the novel, of course, we are never sure whether Mrs. Danvers does burn Manderley, with or without Favell's complicity, or whether it combusts spontaneously of its own incessant masquerades. If du Maurier's Mrs. Danvers were a pyromaniac, she would surely be punishing Maxim for killing Rebecca, not for marrying again: she has no interest in happy endings but only in a single laughing, mocking, boyish woman.

Like his Mrs. Danvers, Hitchcock's Maxim cares only for love and marriage: when he sees his wife outside the burning mansion briskly walking the dog, he collapses with relief in her arms with never a mention of the estate that possesses him in the novel. Donald Spoto's interpretation beams: "The final frames promise new happiness and release from the tyranny of the past for the de Winters" (p. 90), a happiness and release inconceivable in Daphne du Maurier's shackled fictional world. In the film, though, the nice young couple are united in a nuzzling hug more complacent than anything Hitchcock found in du Maurier.

Hitchcock's *Rebecca* cast a long shadow. Its best sequences are incomparable, but its flaccid sentimentality survives even in later adaptations. The most recent *Rebecca*, serialized in the United States on Mobil Masterpiece Theater (1996; dir. Jim O'Brien), is, superficially, truer to the novel's plot in that Charles Dance's Maxim unapologetically kills Rebecca. He expiates at the end—in a clanging echo of *Jane Eyre* that has no relation to du Maurier's novel—by rushing, Rochester-like, into burning Manderley to save mad Mrs. Danvers. Improbably, he lifts hefty Diana Rigg and cripples himself trying to carry her down the fiery stairs. In du Maurier's novel, we never see Manderley burn, nor do we know that Mrs. Danvers is the arsonist. Du Maurier's Maxim does not limp at the end; he is only radically bereaved. But like so many du Maurier characters who find new life on the BBC, this most recent Maxim embodies a lost and cherished England. He sacrifices himself as the epitome of that exclusively English breed, a gentleman. He is stricken by noblesse oblige, not murderous madness.[9]

The BBC Manderley is not an evil house. At the end, the loving wife murmurs, not Daphne du Maurier's haunted exorcism, but a tender prayer to Manderley's ideal potential: "I would not be bitter. I would think of Manderley as it might have been if we could have lived there without fear." This Manderley is a gracious family seat, not the enshrined madness of power. A novel about hate mutates into a pensive story of love and loss.

Hitchcock's *Rebecca* shadowed not only future *Rebecca*s but Joan Fontaine as well. Her later roles reiterated, and romanticized, her haunted Mrs. de Winter. In *Jane Eyre* (1944), she metamorphosed into the Brontë heroine all du Maurier's women are supposed to be at heart: tender, fragile, safely Victorian, clinging to a Rochester (Orson

Welles) who, unlike Olivier's shrunken Maxim, is dashing and expansive. Fontaine's Jane Eyre makes *Rebecca* seem, in memory, more romantic and antiquarian than it is.

In *Frenchman's Creek* (1944), Joan Fontaine played her last du Maurier woman, Lady Dona St. Columb, who abandons her dull husband and picturesque children for a romantic interlude with a pirate. *Frenchman's Creek* is the du Maurier novel closest to a conventional romance, but the film romanticizes it further. Fontaine is swallowed in outrageously ornate costumes and a screaming red wig which may be intended to recall Maureen O'Hara in *Jamaica Inn*; her pirate-lover (Arturo de Cordova) is a piggy-looking man and a dreadful actor; but the dream ship sailing into Turneresque seas and skies is a gorgeous sight that irradiates the actors. Fontaine, more lady than pirate, is miscast as Lady Dona, whose boyish erotic venturesomeness and hatred of her husband bring her closer to Rebecca than to the shrinking Mrs. de Winter. Weighted down by heavy costumes and an uncongenial role, Joan Fontaine obediently plays out her cinematic association with romance, with love and landscape, with a glamorous past, with everything Daphne du Maurier came to stand for and never believed in.

But Joan Fontaine's most galvanizing *Rebecca* spin-off was her performance as the wife in Alfred Hitchcock's *Suspicion* (1941), for which she won an Academy Award. *Suspicion* unleashes the marital terror *Rebecca* suppresses, though *Suspicion* ostensibly reverses *Rebecca*'s dynamic of power: Fontaine plays a society girl who marries a penniless con man (Cary Grant at his most sleekly biting). But despite her wealth, Fontaine's Lina is the same contorted, self-doubting woman as her penniless Mrs. de Winter, while Grant's Johnnie is as mercurial and controlling as Maxim. Maxim's wealth licensed him to command, but Lina's makes her vulnerable to an erratic and greedy husband who, she becomes certain, is going to kill her.

Like *Rebecca*, *Suspicion* steps back, in a tacked-on ending, from making a popular movie star a wife-murderer.[10] But *Suspicion* is pervaded by the domestic terror that Hitchcock's *Rebecca* had deflected to ancillary characters. Joan Fontaine's Lina regards Johnnie with the fascinated revulsion her Mrs. de Winter had reserved for Mrs. Danvers. Olivier's Maxim was a sweet, withdrawn man who never partook of his sinister surroundings, but Cary Grant's Johnnie is as wild and enticing as his car.

The driving scenes in *Suspicion* reprise the scenes that begin *Rebecca*, but here, they are dangerous—as they are in du Maurier's novel, whose narrator remembers fearful excitement driving with Maxim: "This car had the wings of Mercury I thought, for higher yet we climbed, and dangerously fast, and the danger pleased me because it was new to me, because I was young" (p. 28). In Hitchcock's adaptation, Olivier is so composed a driver that these scenes have no charge, but in *Suspicion*, Cary Grant asks wickedly, "Have you ever been kissed in a car?" and Joan Fontaine can't resist. At the climax, Grant careens around the sort of curves Olivier navigated so carefully, embodying all the menace Daphne du Maurier found in men and marriage—the menace Hitchcock tempered. When, in the tacked-on ending, Johnnie turns suddenly on Lina, excoriating her unwholesome mistrust of his thoroughly untrustworthy self, Cary Grant might be Alfred Hitchcock denouncing Daphne du Maurier's fear of men who do not want to look like what they are.[11]

As an anatomy of Gothic marriage, *Suspicion* is the *Rebecca* Hitchcock drew back from making; but if he denied Daphne du Maurier while he was adapting her novel, she infused his later work, and not only *Suspicion.* Hitchcock had more in common with the mordant and paranoid side of Daphne du Maurier than he faced in his sanitized adaptations:[12] as with Johnnie's sexily reckless driving in *Suspicion*, he unleashes du Maurier's images in his non-du Maurier work. His *Strangers on a Train* (1951) has more in common with du Maurier's *Scapegoat*—though du Maurier's novel did not appear until 1957—than did the timid film adaptation. In *Strangers on a Train*, two men collaborate to murder a woman; no clear moral or psychic boundary distinguishes them. Crazy Bruno Antony is eager for the game, while Guy Haines hangs back in terror, but Guy is no more virtuous than Bruno: as a famous tennis player about to marry into society, Guy has everything to lose, while Bruno, an aimless dilettante, has fun and fortune to gain. Mad, mesmerizing Bruno is as much a forbidden part of Guy as, in *The Scapegoat*, wild French Jean is of irreproachable English John.

In du Maurier's earlier *Progress of Julius*, the son inherits the soul of his pacific, wife-murdering father; successive generations of Johns and Henrys absorb each other in *Hungry Hill*; in *My Cousin Rachel*, Ambrose's rages and terrors infest Philip. *Strangers on a Train* seems far from the Daphne du Maurier whom Hitchcock tried to invent; there is no luscious atmosphere, no redemptive romantic love; but its two men, who are not so much distinct characters as tentacles of a shared murder, recapitulate the primary du Maurier relationship. In his indirect way, Hitchcock was Daphne du Maurier's most faithful collaborator, though when he confronts her directly he twists her into submission.

Hitchcock's magnificent *Vertigo* (1958) looks like his most personal work—it features emotionally and psychically crippled men who, with increasing frenzy, twist women into ghostly images—but it is also his most du Maurieresque vision. Its doomed collaboration between an apparent villain and a supposed hero; its amalgam of love, possession, and murder; its mutable San Francisco, alternately foggy and dreadfully bright, like the Manderley of the novel; its Gothic drift toward a lethal romantic past—all of these motifs resurrect the novels Hitchcock would not film directly.

In *Rebecca*'s climactic costume ball, the wife descends the stairs dressed as Maxim's ancestor Lady Caroline de Winter. She doesn't know that she is acting out Mrs. Danvers's obsession to resurrect Rebecca herself, who had dressed as Lady Caroline at the last ball. In the novel, her descent arouses the family's horror: not only is Maxim faced with the wife he has killed, so that the first wife engulfs the second, but both wives summon the returned ancestor Lady Caroline—a terrible, yearned-for climax in the novels of a writer like du Maurier who was possessed by a strangling legacy.

In Hitchcock's *Rebecca*, the wife's descent is flat. Not only does Joan Fontaine look innocuously pretty, not ghostly, in her eighteenth-century costume; we never see this multiple revenant through the eyes of the haunted de Winter family. No one is frightened; when Rebecca's body returns from the sea, the ensuing melodrama upstages the masquerade.

Vertigo, in contrast, spirals in and out of du Maurier's image of a multiple revenant. A nameless woman (Kim Novak) plays a Madeleine Elster possessed by her ancestor Carlotta Valdes, who, like Caroline de Winter, exists only as a romantic portrait. Madeleine's husband hires Scottie (James Stewart), a retired, guilt-stricken detective whose dread of heights had led to the death of a police colleague, to tail the supposed Madeleine. Scottie becomes captivated by the captured woman. Transfixed, he follows her around San Francisco as she follows her relics of the dead Carlotta.

Scottie doesn't know that the possessed Madeleine is an impersonator: his employer, Gavin Elster, has set up Scottie's disability as his alibi in a plot to murder the real Madeleine. Paralyzed by vertigo, Scottie sees the woman he loves throw herself off a tower. After ostensibly recovering from a breakdown, the still-shattered Scottie meets Judy, a blowzy working-class brunette. He sees in her his lost, aimless, ice-blonde Madeleine, and becomes rabid to transform her into his dead beloved—though the viewer has already learned that Judy and Madeleine are the same woman. In his rage to transform Judy, Scottie is himself transformed into a gangly American reincarnation of George du Maurier's foreign wizard Svengali.[13] By the end, both characters are lost in their ghosts. The final reincarnation, in which Judy as Madeleine carelessly puts on Carlotta's necklace, precipitates her final fall and his final paralysis. As in *Rebecca*, a pliant nameless woman puts on an ancestor's costume and is possessed by ancestral ghosts of doom.

A summary of *Vertigo*'s convoluted plot cannot resurrect the dreamlike experience of seeing the film. Scottie's incessant obsessions, the nameless woman's incessant mutations, unmoor the viewer from the beginning. *Vertigo* is Hitchcock's best-known self-dramatization as a possessed filmmaker—Donald Spoto's influential biography, *The Dark Side of Genius*, sees *Vertigo* as his ultimate confession of his need to create and kill blonde actresses—but it is also his ultimate cinematic transmutation of Daphne du Maurier's novels.

Scottie is an oblique du Maurier man. He too is a collaborator, if an unconscious one who never knows that he is performing Elster's murder as du Maurier's Philip Ashley performed Ambrose's. Unlike du Maurier's men, Scottie is a devious killer; his weapon is paralysis, not possessive rage. But falling bodies haunt him, flooding his vision with his obsessions. No adaptation of a Daphne du Maurier novel is as true as *Vertigo* to her possessed storytellers and dislocating perspectives. The unstable San Francisco of *Vertigo*, its swooping bridges and towers, the sudden ascents and descents of its hills, its giant redwoods and sucking sea, anticipate the instability of du Maurier's *House on the Strand*, whose houses and hills are in such spasmodic flux that there is no vantage point even on the land.

It is impossible to know whether Alfred Hitchcock and Daphne du Maurier pirated each other or whether, for all their dissonance, they were kin. The man who left England and the woman who stayed there; the woman who hated America and the man who fed on it; the woman who wrestled with the literary past and the self-styled cinematic innovator and *auteur*—they converged at their hearts while they fought each other in their plots. Finally, though, the man captured the woman, just as he does in du Maurier's novels and Hitchcock's films, for Alfred Hitchcock dubbed himself an artist as Daphne du Maurier never did. Taking advantage of her modesty, he turned her terrible birds into lovebirds.

In its cloistered familial setting, its emphasis on relationships, Hitchcock's *The Birds* is a classic woman's film, but its source is not a traditional woman's story. Daphne du Maurier's brief, blunt tale "The Birds" (1952) is shorn of humanity and short of hope. It is rooted in Cornwall, but its perspective is global.

Some indeterminate shift in nature's balance has caused the world's disparate birds to join forces against the human race. The story begins with a metamorphosis: "On December the third the wind changed overnight and it was winter."[14] Is the sudden freeze an Arctic air shift?

Does it come from Russia—a likely guess in 1952? We know only that the regularity of the seasons has disappeared and so has humanity's future. The birds' aggression has something to do with this shift in nature—Nat Hocken, the story's enterprising but futile hero, figures out that "there was some law the birds obeyed, and it was all to do with the east wind and the tide" (p. 307)—but he can only barricade his family against the inevitable extinction.

In a sense all du Maurier's most powerful novels prophesy the end of England and, thus, of her world. *Rebecca, My Cousin Rachel, The House on the Strand*, her final, acrid *Rule Britannia*—all end with desiccated characters who inherit a drained nation. Even the endings of her historical novels *The King's General* and *Hungry Hill* are pervaded by national as well as personal blight. The central fact of Daphne du Maurier's England is a decomposition consummated in the stark allegory of "The Birds."

Like most of du Maurier's tales, "The Birds" is a distillation of her long, busy novels, and like the novels, it retells a family plot. In 1909, an ancestral voice had prophesied war to great eclat: under the pseudonym "A Patriot," her uncle Guy du Maurier had written a sensational invasion play, *An Englishman's Home*. The play, in which an ordinary English family, the Browns, is taken over by an unspecified enemy, was a rousing call to domestic preparedness. Mr. Brown dies a patriot and hero, as Guy himself would do at the Front in 1915, becoming a symbol of lost integrity to his family.

With typical loyal irreverence, Daphne rewrote her uncle's script. As she described *An Englishman's Home*, "Guy was a soldier, and his play was about civilians who fought in England to defend their homes and their women, and he knew what invasion would mean to us who have never known" (*Gerald: A Portrait*, p. 94). Her Nat Hocken is as ordinary and as brave as Mr. Brown. He too takes care of "his women": his wife (like the wife in *Rebecca*, this good woman has no name) obeys his instructions and asks no questions, helping him shield their buoyant children from awareness of catastrophe. The Hockens' dialogue pays laconic tribute to the gallantry of Guy's Browns:

His wife had made him cocoa and he drank it thirstily. He was very tired.

"All right," he said, smiling, "don't worry. We'll get through." (p. 308)

But in this England, there can be no inspirational example, for no one is left to be inspired. Guy had made audiences love his archetypal British family, Mr. and Mrs. Brown, but Daphne's Hockens are as characterless as her birds. The efficiency with which the birds attack, Nat responds, and the story is told, generates terror without pity.

"The Birds" is cast in the idiom of the Cold War—it is literally a cold story; most of the action takes place during frozen nights—but it throngs with echoes of more benign British catastrophes. The tale not only revises Guy du Maurier's World War I propaganda play, but the characters experience the bird attack by reverting to the rules of World War II. Nat, a disabled veteran, hoards food and boards windows as he had done during the war; he compares his neighbors' inertia to their response to "air raids in the war" (p. 291); he nurses cheering visions of the army, navy, air force, and all their bombs coming to save them; and he huddles with his family around their beacon, the radio (there is no mention of television)—at least until the broadcasts stop, letting us know, obliquely, that London has fallen.

When the BBC fails, we realize that the point of the story is the devastation we don't see: that of "the towns." As Nat explains, "we don't matter so much here. The gulls will serve for us. The others [the other species of birds] go to the towns" (p. 298). One family is left temporarily alive because an English household is inconsequential. As the story ends, Nat and his wife brood about the outside: "Maybe it's the same right through Europe." "Surely America will do something?" (p. 318). The story, like civilization, fades out.

In 1963, America did do something: guided by that transplanted Englishman Alfred Hitchcock, the birds migrated to California, changing their target from time-hallowed domestic fortitude to the complications of love and sex. Du Maurier's story is dark and claustrophobic; the birds attack at night, forcing the Hockens into increasingly cramped domestic spaces. Du Maurier's England is dark even in daytime: "The sky was hard and leaden, and the brown hills that had gleamed in the sun the day before looked dark and bare. The east wind, like a razor, stripped the trees, and the leaves, crackling and dry, shivered and scattered with the wind's blast" (p. 288).

The sun never sets on Hitchcock's California. Bodega Bay, the idyllic seaside village where most of the film is set, is bright even at night. Two women, one dark, one blonde, both in love with the same psychically suspect man, are staying together in a snug cottage. As they prepare for bed, they hear the thud of a bird against the door. Annie, the doomed dark girl, pities the dead bird, assuming it got lost in the dark. Melanie, the film's bright, battered heroine, knows better: "But it isn't dark, Annie; there's a full moon." Like just about everyone in California, Hitchcock's birds are creatures of sex, sun, and space. His most frightening scenes are not claustrophobic but panoramic: the birds come dive-bombing out of a huge sky, filling our vision. Even when Melanie is trapped, like du Maurier's Hockens, in closed spaces—a car, a telephone booth—these spaces are glassed-in, not walled-in. Melanie, and we, can see the panoramic sweep of space, the site of American danger.

Hitchcock not only transplants du Maurier's story, he teases it mercilessly. His fog-oozing *Rebecca* drowned a sharply observed novel. The brightness of *The Birds* is not only a transplantation of du Maurier's bleak England to spacious new America, it is a comic tweaking of du Maurier's grim earnestness.

Du Maurier's birds follow the turn of the tide; Hitchcock's are seemingly on their own. Mitch Brenner, a hero as staunch as Nat Hocken, if more neurotic, explicates a rule independent of moon or tides: "It's like a pattern. They strike, then disappear, and then start massing again." These birds like domesticated spaces. They flock to telephone wires, a gas station, a jungle gym, a yard elaborately decorated for a children's party. As snugly humanized as the movie itself, these birds seem as far from the pull of the tides as is the restaurant that embodies the only tides the movie cares about.

The Tides, a chic café in Bodega Bay, is the setting for Hitchcock's sly bow to his grim source. As the bird attacks are accelerating, Hitchcock breaks the momentum to give us an elaborate set piece of choric comic relief. All sorts of droll eccentrics inhabit The Tides, the most prominent of whom sound evilly like Daphne du Maurier.

A comic drunk who keeps woozily repeating, "It's the end of the world; it's the end of the world," deflates her parable of natural Armageddon. The man is such an ass that he must be wrong, as wrong as the woman who twitters on about ornithology, though, like du Maurier's Nat, Hitchcock's Mrs. Bundy knows all about birds.

Much of the terror of du Maurier's story comes from Nat's ornithological expertise: he knows the birds by their species; he knows these species have never, until the story begins, joined forces. His knowledge of doom comes from his knowledge of birds:

> The tapping went on and on and a new rasping note struck Nat's ear, as though a sharper beak than any hitherto had come to take over from its fellows. He tried to remember the names of birds, he tried to think which species would go for this particular job. It was not the tap of the woodpecker. That would be light and frequent. This was more serious, because if it continued long the wood would splinter as the glass had done. Then he remembered the hawks. Could the hawks have taken over from the gulls? Were there buzzards now upon the sills, using talons as well as beaks? Hawks, buzzards, kestrels, falcons—he had forgotten the birds of prey. He had forgotten the gripping power of the birds of prey. (p. 311)

Hitchcock's Mrs. Bundy knows everything du Maurier knows: "Ornithology happens to be my avocation," she trills. "I have never known birds of different species to flock together. The concept is unimaginable." So said Nat, but knowledge of birds' natural habits was his knowledge of doom. Mrs. Bundy, though, is a sentimental bird lover, claiming that the twittering little dears bring beauty; only humans are aggressors.

Once again, Hitchcock turns Daphne du Maurier into the sentimentalist she wasn't—a sentimentalist who, moreover, wears standard lesbian garb, the same mannish costume Hitchcock gave his female detective novelist and her woman friend in *Suspicion*, the uniform du Maurier will give the psychic sisters in *Don't Look Now*.[15]

Hitchcock doesn't merely change du Maurier's story: he subtly beats it down. Despite the sweeping cinematography, he also makes it shrink. Du Maurier's Cornwall was peripheral to an attack that focused on "the towns," the centers of world civilization, whose decimation we can only imagine. Hitchcock's Bodega Bay is the center of the bird attacks and of the movie's world. The film begins in a bustling San Francisco, where Melanie, and we, see our first ominous gathering of too many gulls, but for the duration of the movie, at least, San Francisco represents safety.

Melanie's father, who owns a San Francisco newspaper, is incredulous when she tells him of the birds' attack on the Bodega Bay School. When the characters remember to turn on the radio—they are too obsessed with each other to focus on it as the Hockens did—they hear bulletins about their own village from a San Francisco reassuringly untouched. One bulletin ends, "On the national scene today, in Washington…" This Washington is not a target like du Maurier's London; it is a familiar distant drone. Just before Mitch drives wounded Melanie to San Francisco, he hears on the car radio: "For the time being, Bodega Bay seems to be the center, though there are reports of minor attacks in Sebastopol and a few on Santa Rosa." Perhaps the birds will fan out after we leave the theater,[16] but we see only the insularity of their attacks on our already inward-turned group of protagonists.

The Birds was disparaged when it came out, but it has become a critical cult film, largely, I think, because it seems to accommodate so many possible readings. Does Melanie's sexual arousal, symbolized by the lovebirds she brings the Brenners, evoke the attacks? Or is Melanie herself some kind of great bird-woman whose presence is an avian command? Hitchcock plays with this possibility when he has a woman in The Tides denounce Melanie as evil and a witch, but since no one in The Tides says anything true, and since Melanie herself is one focus of the attacks, Hitchcock encourages us to look elsewhere, perhaps everywhere.

Does the judgmental Mitch summon the birds as a kind of domestic Judgment Day? Or do they obey the unconscious wishes of his clinging, jealous mother?[17] Or of jealous, lovelorn Annie? Or do they emanate from the psychosexual entanglements among these four? If so, why do they target seemingly sexless children? In one of the only episodes that du Maurier's story and Hitchcock's film share, parents strive to protect their child's school from attack. Du Maurier's birds ignore the school: they are too conversant with the sources of power to bother with children, while in the film's most famous scene, Hitchcock's birds engulf both school and children. Her birds aim at global conquest; his inward-directed invaders swoop to families.

Why, too, do the birds devour some characters (Annie, for instance) and only peck demurely at others (such as Melanie)? Are they lovebirds after all, attacking one pretty little town and its environs to further the emotional growth of chosen characters? By the end, Melanie, like Marnie in Hitchcock's next film, is sufficiently incapacitated by the birds to be loved by a controlling hero.

For devotees of Hitchcock these seem like an infinite range of interpretations, but their range is actually quite narrow. The film nudges us to dwell on a few psychosexual possibilities, a spectrum of love stories. However it lets us read the birds, the humans are amenable to critical psychobabble: the attacks bring Mitch and Melanie to "acceptance of the human need for a relationship grounded in mutual respect and tenderness. It reveals the essentially positive bent of an undermining and ruthless film: in counterpoint to the breaking down of Lydia, the building up of a fertile relationship" (Wood, p. 165).

This reading is probably not wrong, but its reverence for "relationships" shows how feminized Daphne du Maurier's material becomes in Hitchcock's hands. His film, brilliant as it is, is essentially a love story about a chosen couple in a pretty little place. Like his domesticated *Rebecca*, it is just the sort of work a delicate blonde named Daphne du Maurier should have written, but didn't.

Hitchcock's love story makes one realize how loveless du Maurier's "Birds" is. No one is tender; no one has memories; no one says gallant good-byes. None of du Maurier's characters has the power to cause the attack; they merely adjust to it. Hitchcock's *Birds* turns immobilized England into dynamic America and political paranoia into psychosexuality, but du Maurier's tale is larger than Hitchcock's movie because no one in it has time for a love story.

Just as Melanie Daniels is pecked and mangled into male control, so, through her story, is Daphne du Maurier. It is not surprising that du Maurier "hated the film and couldn't understand why Hitchcock had so distorted her story" (Forster, p. 438). One trademark of Hitchcock's later work is his animus toward self-possessed blonde female stars; over and over, his films enthrone them to beat them down. Daphne du Maurier, to whose work he kept returning, may have been his archetypal beaten blonde. Like Svengali's, his obsession turns her into the artist he wants her to be: a perfect woman as he understands the species. But like Svengali's, it is his vision that survives in her name. When du Maurier parrots Hitchcock, she loses herself.

But Alfred Hitchcock isn't the only director to make Daphne du Maurier into a lover. Nicolas Roeg's strange, beautiful adaptation (1973) of her novella *Don't Look Now* (1970) was her favorite film of her work (it is also mine) in that it was the only one to rely, like her fiction, on a subjective camera. As she wrote to Roeg: "I know I make the adaptor's work more difficult by too often writing a story as a narrator or through a single character's mind, which necessitates further invention on the part of the adaptor, and director, to enable a story and its people to come alive, and here you have succeeded admirably, indeed added more depth to unconscious thoughts that might have been my own!"[18]

In Roeg's *Don't Look Now*, there are no bird's-eye shots of eaten corpses or battered women; the camera sees what the lost John Baxter sees, a cold, crumbling, incoherent Venice, teeming with bridges and alleys that seemingly lead only into darkness. I suspect that unlike

Hitchcock, Roeg had no interest in Daphne du Maurier or her work. Her fame had faded by the 1970s, but film had caught up to the spooky narrative perspectives she had used since the 1930s. An experimental director, Nicolas Roeg saw, through his camera, an inherently Daphne du Maurieresque world. Technically compatible as they were, however, Roeg, like Hitchcock and her other adapters, turns a novella about hate into a movie about love.

Like most other adaptations, *Don't Look Now* is faithful to du Maurier's plot. Both fiction and film feature a bereaved young English couple traveling in Venice; they meet two spiritualist sisters who claim to have seen their dead daughter. The sisters assert that the child has come back to warn John, the husband—who, they insist, is also psychic—that if he remains in Venice, his life is in danger. Nevertheless, when Laura returns to England, John remains in Venice, where he becomes increasingly drunk and lost. In his befuddlement, remembering his dead daughter, he follows a red-cloaked child up a flight of stairs. The child turns out to be a homicidal dwarf who murders him. In both the novella and the movie, the psychic husband has denied or misconstrued both his own visions and the women who understand them. His ignominious death is a failure of faith, or a failure to look at what women see.

Du Maurier's story is haunted, and not only by the unseen ghost of a dead child, but also by images from du Maurier's own past. In Roeg's film, the psychic sisters are dithery and maternal. They meet because Heather, the sighted sister, cannot remove a speck of dust from her eye—the visionary sister is blind—and needs Laura's help to extract it. "You do remind me of my daughter," Heather says tenderly; they are sympathetic to Laura's bereavement because Heather is still mourning a dead child. When John escorts Wendy, the blind sister, to her hotel, she clings to him and murmurs, "It's so nice to have a man." "He's been looking after me," she coos to Heather. When John blunders into the streets and his death, Wendy cries out in the throes of a vision, "Fetch him back! Let him not go!" Heather obediently, but futilely, trots after him.

In du Maurier's story, though, the weird sisters are themselves ghosts of a child-free community of women Daphne remembered from the 1920s. They wear, not the clunky pins and dowdy skirts Roeg gives them, but a mannish uniform John remembers with animosity from his mother's generation: "She would be in her middle sixties, he supposed, the masculine shirt with collar and tie, sports jacket, gray tweed skirt coming to mid-calf. Grey stockings and laced black shoes."[19] John goes on to assure the reader, or himself, that some of these mannish women are married to men they adore, but the specter has risen. He fears the sisters not only because they are psychic; he is haunted by their gruff self-sufficiency (neither sister gets a cinder in her eye, or has children, or twitters about how good it is to have a man to take care of her, or wails at John's fate, or runs to save him). He is obsessed by a facetious fear that they are men in drag, out to abduct and corrupt his wife.

Daphne du Maurier's daughter remembered such a female couple from her childhood at Menabilly, imagining innocently that only their governess, not her mother, was drawn to them:

> In the heart of the Menabilly woods was an old cottage called Southcott, once a dwelling for game-keepers. It stood in a small clearing, a little way off the old drive. During our play, we always gave this place a wide berth. Isolated as it was, two elderly ladies lived there, a Miss Phillips and her companion, Miss Wilcox. The former had been private secretary to old Dr. Rashleigh, the owner of Mena. Kits and I thought the couple most sinister, this belief elaborated by Bing [Daphne] with her usual make-believe stories of their life. Rumour had it that they were spiritualists.
>
> If we were biking in the park we would sometimes see the two women return from shopping, walking arm in arm towards the entrance in the park to the old drive. It was a fair way to have to go, and once we biked up to them and asked if they would like some help with their bags. Their black mongrel dog stood guard, low growls coming from its open jaws. Miss Phillips,

her hair very white in the sunlight, turned her mystical-looking blue eyes on us and bowed slightly, a faint smile twitching her lips as if she thought our offer amusing. It was Miss Wilcox, tall and stout, with her thick grey hair wound in plaits round her ears, who spoke: "Be off with you young scamps, you haven't the strength," and she peered at us through the thick pebble glasses and laughed loudly, a deep, harsh sound which made their dog bark.[20]

Miss Phillips and Miss Wilcox look exactly like the weird sisters in du Maurier's *Don't Look Now*, whose blind sister also has very white hair and "mystical-looking blue eyes." Like Miss Phillips and Miss Wilcox, du Maurier's sisters are not the harmless eccentrics they become in the movie; they are the residue of a daring generation of self-sufficient women who took men's names and privileges while following Spiritualism, a woman's religion.

In 1920s Paris, that trend-setting couple Radclyffe Hall and Una Troubridge lived in a Spiritualist ménage à trois with Radclyffe Hall's former lover, who had died but remained part of the household through continual seances. In advanced 1920s circles, Spiritualism cemented the bond among women who renamed and reconceived themselves (the sisters in du Maurier's novella, unlike their cinematic counterparts, admit to no names). No wonder visionary, myopic John is afraid to look at them.

When Daphne du Maurier was young, Spiritualism was perceived as a woman's religion, progressive and feminist; thus when John fears that Laura will be infected by the sisters' vision, he not only worries about her sanity but, like many men in the 1970s, he fears that feminists will witch away his woman. The child Christine is not du Maurier's only ghost: the old ladies who see and hear her, specters of a self-determining generation, are more menacing still to the story's solitary man.

Roeg obliterates the female connotations of Spiritualism by absorbing it into the Catholicism that pervades his movie. Heather tells Laura humbly that "second sight is a gift from the good Lord, who sees all things." As evidence, Roeg makes John a skilled church restorer (not an aimless tourist, as he is in the story), working for a meditative bishop who also has second sight: as John is being killed, not only does Wendy cry out, but the bishop sits up suddenly in bed. Presumably the good bishop is there to legitimize the moaning Wendy. Catholicism suffuses Roeg's *Don't Look Now* with an aura of ornate male solemnity that rescues John from a woman's religion.

John's doom is reinforced and given magnitude not only by the Church: symphonic visual patterns dominate the movie, all of which are ominous portents. Shots of the water in which Christine drowns repeat themselves in Venice, and so does the broken glass present at her drowning; the color red is so insistent a motif that it almost takes precedence over the human story. Christine is wearing a red raincoat; the color red floods a defective slide John is studying, and he mystically knows of his daughter's death. Red floods our vision in Venice; Roeg sometimes cuts to red for no narrative reason, but to warn us, allowing us to see more than the characters can.

These sumptuous fate motifs align John with a majestic destiny absent in du Maurier's story, where his own inept pig-headedness drives him to doom. Roeg further dignifies John's fate by adding a scene where he nearly dies of a freak accident while he is on a scaffold examining a mosaic. John has more magnitude than he does in the novella—not only does his dead daughter care about him, but so do the Catholic establishment, all the film's women, and the pattern of the universe itself—but, like the noblest heroes of mythology, he can do nothing to affect his own death.

Like most of du Maurier's fiction, *Don't Look Now* is pervaded by sexual antagonism. Within the family, the dead daughter "meant everything" to Laura; she is relatively indifferent to her "tough" son (p. 12). The Spiritualist sisters and the ghost of her daughter do draw Laura away from John, who, unable to speak Italian, weaves around Venice in an angry fog until his fatal end. Du Maurier's John is increasingly alone, while Roeg's is watched over by solicitous women, by spiritual men, and by patterns of destiny.

Roeg's movie, moreover, is set in a fashionably unisex ambience. Christine and her brother have matching long curly hair, as do Julie

Christie's Laura and Donald Sutherland's John. Visually, *Don't Look Now* is a romantic evocation of the affinity between men and women. John in the story sees Laura's grief as pathological; John in the movie has a premonition, runs to the pond where Christine has drowned, lifts her body, and roars with anguish. Grief in Roeg's movie is shared, like food and hairstyles. Nothing can drive Donald Sutherland's John and Julie Christie's Laura apart but destiny and death.

Du Maurier's John is a terrible tourist who can't speak Italian; orders inedible food because he doesn't understand the menu; gets lost because he bumptiously pretends that he knows where he's going. Roeg's John is in Venice, not as a tourist, but to do important and interesting work there; his Italian is superb; until the destined end, he is a masterful traveler as well as a tender husband.

Roeg's film is, at its heart, a rapturous celebration of married love. Most viewers have forgotten its ghost story, but its sex scene remains indelible. Roeg inserts in the middle of the movie a lingering lovemaking sequence that flashes intermittently forward to the couple's dressing and dinner, suffusing these mundane actions with a tender erotic glow. Echoing John's psychic flashes into a tragic future, this famous sequence spreads its romantic warmth through the movie, overwhelming the hostility at the heart of du Maurier's *Don't Look Now*.

Du Maurier's original love-making scene is devoid of mutuality. John feels only "such blessed relief after all those weeks of restraint" (p. 19). Roeg's enhancement of this curt sentence adds emotional depth, making us care about the characters and mourn their separation, but it is a love scene Daphne du Maurier never wrote and would never have written.

Horner and Zlosnik feel, and I agree, that *Don't Look Now* is du Maurier's "last successful completed work" (p. 173). Like many last works, it is a ghost play, haunted not only or even primarily by a dead child but by a dead generation in a lost city. In Roeg's *Don't Look Now*, we see an off-season Venice, cold, dark, and empty, but du Maurier's Venice is flooded with tourists and, for the author, with memories.

Her code name for lesbianism was "Venetian." Twenty years earlier, she had written provocatively to Ellen Doubleday: "I glory in my Venice, when I am in a Venice mood, and forget about it when I am not. The only chip is the dreary knowledge that there can never be Venice with you" (quoted in Forster, p. 255). A story haunted by vanished women—Radclyffe Hall and her Spiritualist circle, du Maurier's own boy-self, an Ellen Doubleday who never came—becomes in Roeg's movie a romantic elegy to married love.

Male directors may not deliberately falsify Daphne du Maurier, but if we know her through their movies, we don't know her at all. Alfred Hitchcock, Nicolas Roeg, and the others soften the works they adapt by adding to du Maurier's stark vision love stories she never conceived. These gifted directors not only beautify du Maurier for the movies, they feminize her as well, turning her impersonal, almost inhuman tales into the romances her admirers wish she had written.

7

"Je Reviens"

It is always a lovely prospect to write The End of a book—or a writer, or a life—but like Rebecca, who prophetically named her boat *Je Reviens*, Daphne du Maurier seems never to end. She can only return, and for me, at least, she always has. Bringing her back brings me back to times in my life when I read her obsessively and didn't, until now, understand her protean fascination. Bringing her back is also the right tribute to a woman who appreciated ghosts, who faced down memories, and who is now kept alive in the ghostly medium of movies.

She possessed me first that long-ago summer at camp in Maine, and she returned many years later, when I was having a strangely camp-like semester in Seattle. By 1989, I was no longer a grumpy camper but a happy scholar, on leave from my contained Philadelphia life to become a visiting professor at the University of Washington. At camp, I was supposed to be active and busy playing jolly games, but I remember spending most of my time in a reverie, reading and gazing at spooky landscapes. At the University of Washington, I was supposed to be, I think, a resource for the community, but my main memory of that time involves reading and contemplating menacing skies. My six months in the Pacific Northwest, like my summers in camp, were an amorphous interlude away from my usual routines.

In 1989, Seattle had not yet been discovered by easterners like me: even Starbucks coffee was still a local secret. The city seemed to me marvelously strange. Since my academic routine was flexible, I spent many days walking about in the muzzly fog, climbing and descending big hills, contemplating the web of lakes that played around them, drifting through piles of colossal octopuses and squid at Pike Place Market, and exploring the city's boundless and wonderful used book stores. There, I found more Daphne du Maurier fiction than I knew existed. I dived in once again.

Daphne du Maurier still seemed to me a guilty escape, not a legitimate subject, but reading her in Seattle, a city that seemed to me as eerie as she was, brought her to a new kind of life: she seemed in place. Though I think I read *Rebecca* for the first time during my Seattle immersion, du Maurier seemed farther than ever from escapist romance. I had just written two books on the Victorian theater and theatricality; the seminar I was teaching featured *Trilby*; and so du Maurier came alive within a context of Victorian fantasy, masquerade, and ontological play.

Reading her in Seattle, I began to see how powerfully her inheritance involved the century in which I vicariously lived. My Victorian England is (I hope) built on learning and thought, but it is still, in part, a sort of inaccessible Oz. For Daphne du Maurier, suffused in her unknown grandfather's inheritance, Victorian England was an inescapable dream that clung to her. Energized and haunted by her role as heiress of a dynasty, she confronted her Victorian endowment with loyal resistance.

Because her imagination of herself was dynastic, not lost and alone, she never wrote romances as most people understand them today. Nevertheless, she is, in her way, indisputably a woman writer because like all durable women she fights the tradition she inherits, infusing it with her own skepticism and despair. Her combativeness is her female insignia. Her supposedly feminine fantasies, most of which are dark and, like the hills of Seattle, vertiginous, are weapons against absorption by great men and their past.

It seems I always dive into Daphne du Maurier during respites from my predictable life. I did at last come home to write about her; this book took shape in the cozy jumble of my Philadelphia study, whose every corner and mire of papers I know. But writing it did bring back the elation of unfamiliar places, and also the apprehension of being lost in them.

I hope this book has explored Daphne du Maurier without explaining her away, letting her, too, remain an unfamiliar place. During her life, she never spilled into confession, keeping to herself the fear and strangeness that were hers alone. After her death, as long as she remains elusive, she can still return.

ى   ى   ى

Works by Daphne du Maurier

Novels

The Loving Spirit (1931); *I'll Never Be Young Again* (1932); *The Progress of Julius* (1933); *Jamaica Inn* (1936); *Rebecca* (1938); *Frenchman's Creek* (1942); *Hungry Hill* (1943); *The King's General* (1946); *The Parasites* (1949); *My Cousin Rachel* (1951); *Mary Anne* (1954); *The Scapegoat* (1957); *Castle Dor*, with Arthur Quiller-Couch (1962); *The Glass-Blowers* (1963); *The Flight of the Falcon* (1965); *The House on the Strand* (1969); *Rule Britannia* (1972)

Biographies and Memoirs

Gerald: A Portrait (1934); *The Du Mauriers* (1937); *Come Wind, Come Weather* (1940); (ed.), *The Young George du Maurier: A Selection of His Letters, 1860-1867* (1951); *The Infernal World of Branwell Brontë* (1960); *Vanishing Cornwall* (1967); *Golden Lads: Anthony Bacon, Francis and Their Friends* (1975); *The Winding Stair: Francis Bacon, His Rise and Fall* (1976); *Growing Pains: The Shaping of a Writer* (U.S. title: *Myself When Young*) (1977); *The Rebecca Notebook and Other Memories* (1980)

Plays

The Years Between (1945); *September Tide* (1949)

Collections of Stories

The Apple Tree (1952); *Kiss Me Again, Stranger* (1952); *Happy Christmas* (1953); *Early Stories* (1955); *The Breaking Point* (1959); *Don't Look Now* (1970); *Not After Midnight* (1971); *Echoes from the Macabre* (1976); *The Rendezvous and Other Stories* (1980); *Classics from the Macabre* (1987)

ی

Notes

Chapter 1. Reading Furtively, by Flashlight

1. Daphne du Maurier, *The Scapegoat* (1957; rpt. New York: Pocket Books, 1966), p. 2.

2. Daphne du Maurier, *Hungry Hill* (New York: Doubleday, Doran, 1944), p. 54.

3. Du Maurier's disdain for the Charlotte Brontë whose heir she was supposed to be may flash out in the name of the simpiest, most angelic wife in *Hungry Hill*: Katherine Eyre.

4. The same vision underlies Émile Zola's twenty-volume saga of a decaying family, *Les Rougon-Macquart: The Natural and Social History of a Family Under the Second Empire (1871-93)*. There are many Zolaesque moments in *Hungry Hill*, particularly the recurrent feudal ceremonies spoiled by drunkenness and greed, but Zola, like Mann, has a clear ideal of heroism, though heroes are impossible in a debased age. The skeptical woman writer has no interest in greatness. She is concerned only with power.

5. Margaret Forster, *Daphne du Maurier: The Secret Life of the Renowned Story-teller* (New York: Doubleday, 1993), p. 175.

6. Forster, pp. 435 n. 7, 167.

7. Daphne du Maurier, *Myself When Young: The Shaping of a Writer* (1977; rpt. New York: Avon Books, 1978), p. 32.

Chapter 2. The Men in Her Life

1. Quoted in Leonée Ormond, *George Du Maurier* (London: Routledge and Kegan Paul, 1969), p. 68.

2. George du Maurier, *Peter Ibbetson* (New York and London: Harper & Brothers, 1891), p. 83.

3. George du Maurier, *Trilby* (1894; rpt. New York: Dover, 1994), p. 11.

4. Ormond, pp. 142, 151-53.

5. George du Maurier, *The Martian, Harper's Magazine*, 1896-97, X, p. 193.

6. Daphne du Maurier, "The Young George du Maurier," in *The Rebecca Notebook and Other Memories* (New York: Doubleday, 1980), pp. 222-33.

7. Daphne du Maurier, *The Du Mauriers* (New York: Doubleday, Doran, 1937), p. 114.

8. Daphne du Maurier, *Gerald: A Portrait* (1934; rpt. New York: Pocket Books, 1963), p. 115.

9. Quoted in Forster, p. 422.

10. According to James Harding, *Gerald du Maurier: The Last Actor-Manager* (London: Hodder & Stoughton, 1989), p. 57.

11. Flavia Leng, *Daphne du Maurier: A Daughter's Memoir* (Edinburgh: Mainstream Publishing, 1994), pp. 89–91.

12. Quoted in Forster, p. 222.

13. Martyn Shallcross, *The Private World of Daphne du Maurier* (New York: St. Martin's Press, 1991), p. 15.

14. Daphne du Maurier, "The Old Man," in *Kiss Me Again, Stranger* (1952; rpt. New York: Dell, 1987), p. 224.

15. In a distraught letter written during the crisis precipitated by Tommy's affair and subsequent nervous breakdown, she cast her husband somewhat more flatteringly as father rather than son: "The Old Man was Moper's jealousy of Boo [their son Kit], and his unconscious wish to destroy him" (quoted in Forster, p. 423). Candid as it seems, though, this supposedly confessional letter never mentions the activities of the boy in the box.

16. Quoted in Forster, pp. 221-22.

17. Radclyffe Hall, *The Well of Loneliness* (1928; rpt. New York: Anchor Books, 1990), p. 72.

18. Quoted in Forster, p. 222.

19. Terry Castle perpetuates this tradition of incantatory occultism by dedicating her account of Radclyffe Hall "To Stephen, With Love." See her *Noël Coward and Radclyffe Hall: Kindred Spirits* (New York: Columbia University Press, 1996).

20. In *The Apparitional Lesbian: Female Homosexuality and Modern Culture* (New York: Columbia University Press, 1993), Terry Castle argues seductively that Spiritualism was intrinsic to lesbians who were "ghosted" by a hostile culture–pushed "in the shadows, in the margins, hidden from history, out of sight, out of mind, a wanderer in the dusk" (p. 2)–and who thus continually sought to materialize themselves.

21. Quoted in Lillian Faderman, *Odd Girls and Twilight Lovers: A History of Lesbian Life in Twentieth-Century America* (1991; rpt. New York: Penguin Books, 1992), p. 341 n. 30.

Chapter 3. Family Chronicler

1. Nina Auerbach, *Ellen Terry, Player in Her Time* (1987; rpt. Philadelphia: University of Pennsylvania Press, 1997).

2. She was an assiduous student of others' families. In addition to her use of Christopher Puxley's family history for *Hungry Hill*, she pillaged the letters of the

Slade family in Cornwall for her first novel, a saga misleadingly called *The Loving Spirit*. Her biography of Branwell Brontë is a powerful appendage to the well-studied family history of the Brontës. *Golden Lads* (1975) and *The Winding Stair* (1976) are exhaustive if plodding reconstructions of the history of Anthony and Francis Bacon in the sixteenth century.

3. *The Du Mauriers*, p. 304.

4. Daphne du Maurier, *The Glass-Blowers* (New York: Avon Books, 1963), p. 23.

5. The theatrical Delaney siblings in *The Parasites* probably owe some of their ingrown existence to Glass clan; they too are precious isolates in a banal world; but, as the title demonstrates, du Maurier's parasites have a sardonic self-knowledge, and a hardy, opportunistic will to survive, missing from Salinger's rarefied spirits.

6. Daphne du Maurier, *Mary Anne* (1954; rpt. New York: Avon Books, 1973), p. 3.

7. Forster, p. 8.

8. George du Maurier, *Peter Ibbetson*, p. 291.

9. Daphne du Maurier, "The Apple Tree," in *Kiss Me Again, Stranger* (New York: Doubleday, 1952).

10. Daphne du Maurier, *Rebecca* (1938; rpt. New York: Avon Books, 1971), p. 36.

11. Daphne du Maurier, "The Little Photographer," in *Kiss Me Again, Stranger*.

12. Daphne du Maurier, "Ganymede," in *The Breaking Point* (New York: Doubleday, 1959), p. 98.

13. Daphne du Maurier, *The House on the Strand* (Middlesex: Penguin Books, 1969), p. 83.

14. Maternal detachment was, in the 1930s, a virtue. See Alison Light, *Forever England: Femininity, Literature, and Conservatism Between the Wars* (London: Routledge, 1991), p. 124: "With a less romantic sense of childhood, with relatively little by way of child-oriented consumerism, and as yet no languages of 'teenage' or 'adolescence,' it is adulthood which in the 1930s is at a premium for children and grown-ups alike."

15. George du Maurier, *Trilby*, p. 248.

16. Daphne du Maurier, *The Parasites* (New York: Doubleday, 1950), p. 47.

17. Daphne du Maurier, "The Menace," in *The Breaking Point*, p. 200.

Chapter 4. Life as a Man

1. Fear, it seems, makes woman writers better men. Such tales of terror as *The Lifted Veil*, by George Eliot, and "The Eyes," by Edith Wharton, feature haunted male narrators more dimensional than the men in their supposedly realistic novels. By this rule, though, *Don't Look Now*, Daphne du Maurier's occult novella about a haunted man traveling in Venice to his doom, should be a more successful male impersonation than her novels, but this well-known tale seems to me a shade

thinner than the novels, more interested in exposing its protagonist than in living with him.

2. *A Room of One's Own* (1929; rpt. New York: Harbinger Books, 1957), p. 79. Alison Light makes this association between Woolf and du Maurier in *Forever England*, p. 192.

3. Quoted in Forster, p. 222.

4. Daphne du Maurier, *Monte Verità*, in *Kiss Me Again, Stranger*.

5. Quoted in Forster, p. 257.

6. Daphne du Maurier, "The Matinee Idol" (1973), in *The Rebecca Notebook*, p. 238.

7. Daphne du Maurier, *The Infernal World of Branwell Brontë* (1960; rpt. Middlesex: Penguin Books, 1972), p. 16.

8. *Mary Anne*, p. 358.

9. Daphne du Maurier, "A Border-Line Case," in *Don't Look Now* (New York: Dell, 1985), pp. 161-230.

10. "The Young George du Maurier," in *The Rebecca Notebook*, p. 225.

11. Technically, since his mother is Gentile, Julius is as well, but in Daphne du Maurier's family myth, Judaism, like everything else, is transmitted through the potent paternal line.

12. Daphne du Maurier, *The Progress of Julius* (New York: Doubleday, Doran, 1933), p. 135.

13. Zola's working notes quoted in Frederick Brown, *Zola: A Life* (Baltimore: Johns Hopkins University Press, 1995), p. 264.

14. In 1994, Arrow Books published a new, expurgated edition in which the novel was re-titled *Julius* and shorn of language the editors considered anti-Semitic. See Avril Horner and Sue Zlosnik, *Daphne du Maurier: Writing, Identity and the Gothic Imagination* (New York: St. Martin's Press, 1998), p. 201, n. 57.

15. George du Maurier, *Peter Ibbetson*, pp. 126-27.

16. George du Maurier, *Trilby*, p. 337.

17. Like all Daphne du Maurier's good women, Rachel Sangaletti is, on the surface, all-giving. Far from demanding something for nothing, "she asks nothing, she demands nothing." *My Cousin Rachel* (New York: Doubleday, 1951), p. 71.

18. *My Cousin Rachel* uses the word "cousin" with the same sexy suggestiveness as does the strangulating husband/narrator in "Andrea del Sarto." In *Rebecca*, Rebecca's lewd, insinuating cousin Favell makes of cousinage a synonym for obscenity. *Rebecca* also makes mordant play with Browning's "Porphyria's Lover" in the good wife's last nightmare: she mutates into Rebecca, and her husband Maxim, like Browning's narrator, strangles her with her own serpentine hair.

19. See Horner and Zlosnik, pp. 133-35, for an account of Gothic foreignness in *My Cousin Rachel*.

20. William Thackeray, *Vanity Fair* (1848; rpt. Middlesex: Penguin Books, 1968), p. 622.

21. *The Flight of the Falcon* was published in 1965, making Daphne du Maurier prescient in exploiting student unrest just as it began. The student revolution, as it

came to be called, did not penetrate general awareness until the later 1960s.

22. According to Forster, pp. 336-37, du Maurier saw the novel less as thriller than as disguised personal allegory. I take *The Flight of the Falcon* as an allegory of her own potential submergence in her alluring genealogy.

23. Daphne du Maurier, *The Flight of the Falcon* (New York: Doubleday, 1965), p. 245.

24. *House on the Strand,* p. 91.

Chapter 5. *Rebecca* and Romance

1. Daphne du Maurier, *Frenchman's Creek* (New York: Pocket Books, 1942), p. 153.

2. See Janice A. Radway, *Reading the Romance: Women, Patriarchy, and Popular Literature,* 2nd ed. (Chapel Hill: University of North Carolina Press, 1991), p. 105.

3. "Despite the fact that these [romance] novels span forty years, from 1942 to 1982, one thing remains constant: women and girls' lives begin and should end at home." Linda K. Christian-Smith, *Becoming a Woman Through Romance* (New York: Routledge, 1990), p. 78.

4. Radway is indeterminate on du Maurier as a romance writer. She claims that the persistent success of *Rebecca* as a "gothic" inspired the lucrative chains of women's paperback romances that proliferate to this day (p. 31). Radway never distinguishes "gothic" from "romance," though she does trace a shift in appeal through the twentieth century from dangerous heroes to tenderer, more maternal lovers. For the sake of clarity if not accuracy, I shall continue to call Daphne du Maurier's female-centered novels "romances" because most readers assume that's what they are.

5. *New York Times,* April 20, 1989.

6. The best recent critical books on du Maurier—Alison Light's Marxist account of the British 1930s, *Forever England: Femininity, Literature, and Conservatism Between the Wars,* and Avril Horner and Sue Zlosnik's psychoanalytic *Daphne du Maurier: Writing, Identity, and the Gothic Imagination*—assume that *Rebecca* is her central work, though in the thirty productive years that followed, du Maurier produced nothing akin to that eccentric book. Both critical books seem uneasy with du Maurier's many male-centered works. Light suggests that they evade the central problem of female sexuality, while for Horner and Zlosnik, they are not a triumph but a symptom of du Maurier's fundamental anxiety about the boundaries of the self.

7. *Gerald: A Portrait,* p. 185.

8. Daphne du Maurier, *Jamaica Inn* (New York: Pocket Books, 1936), pp. 262-63.

9. *Rebecca,* p. 53.

10. Charlotte Brontë, *Jane Eyre* (1847; rpt. Middlesex: Penguin Books, 1966), p. 475.

11. Daphne du Maurier, *The King's General* (1946; rpt. London: Victor Gollancz, 1992), p. 54.

12. *Progress of Julius*, p. 47.

13. *Parasites*, p. 69.

14. Obviously, in the England of the 1940s and 1950s, Daphne du Maurier had no access to books like *Our Bodies, Ourselves*. But though we now know that Celia didn't need surgery for fibroid tumors, du Maurier's persistent vision of women—"there's something gone wrong inside"—is more metaphysical than medical.

15. Horner and Zlosnik, p. 69.

16. Light, p. 165.

17. Daphne du Maurier, *The Loving Spirit* (New York: Doubleday, Doran, 1931), p. 18.

18. Emily Brontë, *Wuthering Heights* (1847; rpt. Middlesex: Penguin Books, 1965), pp. 120-21.

19. Patsy Stoneman enumerates the many plot echoes between the two novels, but she elides the fact that Jane Eyre enters Thornfield as a servant and graduates to becoming a wife; the second Mrs. de Winter is already a wife when she enters Manderley, but a wife who is in servitude and who progresses at the end to the role of traveling companion with which she began. See Patsy Stoneman, *Brontë Transformations: The Cultural Dissemination of "Jane Eyre" and "Wuthering Heights"* (New York: Prentice Hall, 1996), pp. 99-101.

20. Michelle A. Massé also finds Jane Eyre more inspiring than the second Mrs. de Winter, as typified by Jane's refusal to empathize with Rochester's brutality toward his first wife: "Where the protagonist of *Rebecca* merges with Maxim as he narrates the murder of a vilified other woman, Jane cannot do so. The man she loves is in effect beating another woman: she neither calls it love nor justifies it through righteous hate; she can and does silently note it." Michelle A. Massé, *In the Name of Love: Women, Masochism, and the Gothic* (Ithaca: Cornell University Press, 1992), p. 228.

21. Michelle Massé suggests shrewdly, p. 181, that Rebecca's money as well as her taste were necessary to create Manderley in its sumptuous heyday. She suggests, too, that despite Rebecca's famous malformed uterus, Maxim may be impotent as well as impecunious. Indeed, there is no hint of the second Mrs. de Winter's producing an heir, though subordinate characters keep eyeing her figure hopefully. The couple's obstetrical problems continue in Susan Hill's superfluous sequel, *Mrs. de Winter* (1993).

22. Daphne du Maurier, "The Blue Lenses," in *The Breaking Point*, p. 86.

23. Joanna Russ, "Somebody's Trying to Kill Me and I Think It's My Husband: The Modern Gothic," in *To Write Like a Woman: Essays in Feminism and Science Fiction* (Bloomington: Indiana University Press, 1995), p. 108.

Chapter 6. Movie Star

1. Robin Wood, *Hitchcock's Films Revisited* (New York: Columbia University Press, 1989), p. 74.

2. *Scapegoat,* p. 6.

3. *Gerald: A Portrait,* p. 185.

4. *Jamaica Inn,* pp. 262-63.

5. Like virtually all Hitchcock critics, Donald Spoto assumes that the simpleminded novel needed the Master's touch to be made Art: Hitchcock, he claims, "fashioned a script with breadth and nuance, with wit and universality beyond the straightforwardness of du Maurier's plot." Donald Spoto, *The Art of Alfred Hitchcock: Fifty Years of His Motion Pictures* (New York: Doubleday, 1979), p. 89. I suspect that Spoto never bothered to read the novel, so fatuous does Hitchcock's cinematic parody make it look.

6. *Rebecca,* p. 53.

7. Forster, pp. 137-38.

8. Horner and Zlosnik make this point, claiming that by missing the journey, the wife remains infantilized, while in the novel she acquires initiative and independence; see pp. 106-7. By closing the wife in the burning Manderley, Hitchcock also creates a romantic situation alien to du Maurier's novel, allowing Maxim to wring his hands with worry about his wife rather than mourning his estate.

9. I remember seeing an earlier BBC *Rebecca* during the 1980s with authentically creepy performances by Jeremy Brett and Joanna David, but I wantonly recorded over my videotape and cannot now remember whether it too is steeped in nostalgia.

10. In the source, Anthony Berkeley Cox's novel *Before the Fact,* the shady husband does kill his wife. When he changed the plot to exonerate Cary Grant and indict Joan Fontaine, Hitchcock fell back on his reliable antagonists, vain actors and benighted producers in thrall to a philistine Production Code. As with *Rebecca,* though, his shrinking from actual wife-murder came from his own evasions: unlike the Daphne du Maurier he patronized, the early Hitchcock was more comfortable dwelling on morbid women than confronting violent men. See Donald Spoto, *The Dark Side of Genius: The Life of Alfred Hitchcock* (1983; New York: Ballantine Books, 1984), pp. 253-54.

11. At least in his early book on Hitchcock, Donald Spoto turns the false ending into a happy one, for male spectators at least: "The same scene concludes *Notorious, The Birds* and *Marnie*: a man takes control and drives a beleaguered woman toward the prospect of a new life." *Art of Alfred Hitchcock,* p. 122. *To Catch a Thief* (1955) mocks this idyll of male control by making a wild woman driver, Grace Kelly, lurch Cary Grant around perilous curves.

12. Tania Modleski makes this point in *The Woman Who Knew Too Much: Hitchcock and Feminist Theory* (New York and London: Methuen, 1988), pp. 45-54.

13. Hitchcock regularly played Svengali when he wanted to terrify actresses, but the role overcame him during *Rebecca.* According to Joan Fontaine, "He seemed

to want total possession of me....He was a Svengali. He controlled me totally" (Spoto, *Dark Side,* p. 126).

14. Daphne du Maurier, "The Birds" (1952), rpt. *Echoes from the Macabre* (1976; rpt. New York: Avon Books, 1978), p. 283.

15. If Hitchcock uses Mrs. Bundy to caricature one incarnation of du Maurier, might his cool, self-possessed blondes, who are increasingly broken down as his films evolve, reflect du Maurier's other, feminine face? In *The Birds*, Tippi Hedren's elegant Melanie handles a boat as deftly as Rebecca, perhaps even as well as Daphne du Maurier; but Melanie is too shattered at the end to drive her own car.

16. Spoto, *Art of Alfred Hitchcock*, p. 394, claims that Hitchcock considered ending the film with the group's final arrival at a Golden Gate bridge covered with malevolent birds, but that wisely rejected ending belongs in a different film.

17. Margaret M. Horowitz makes this claim in "The Birds: A Mother's Love" (1982), rpt. in *A Hitchcock Reader*, ed. Marshall Deutelbaum and Leland Poague (Ames: Iowa State University Press, 1986), pp. 279-87.

18. Quoted in Shallcross, p. 151.

19. Daphne du Maurier, *Don't Look Now* (1970), rpt. in *Echoes from the Macabre*, p. 11.

20. Leng, p. 107.

Acknowledgments

When an author claims that her book would not have been written without others' help, it is usually sanctimonious simpering, but in the case of this book, it is true. Since I was a child, Daphne du Maurier has been one star of my secret reading, but I never would have thought of writing about her without two editors' matchmaking ingenuity.

When George Stade invited me to contribute an entry on Daphne du Maurier to his monumental series of literary encyclopedias, *British Writers,* I was thrilled to be writing officially about an author who had always obsessed me—especially since Margaret Forster's superb biography, *Daphne du Maurier: The Secret Life of the Renowned Storyteller,* had just appeared in America. I could not have written about Daphne du Maurier had Margaret Forster not done so; I would not have written about her without George Stade.

A year or so later, Jerry Singerman, editor at the University of Pennsylvania Press, suggested I inaugurate his new series, Personal Takes, with a book on Daphne du Maurier. As always, I was guiltily elated to return to her—but as I discovered her unique complexity, I lost my guilt and became simply elated. As I thrashed around in the welter of material and memories that became this book, Jerry proved to be a young editor of the old school—that is, an editor full of curiosity who actually reads what I write, argues about it, and searches out new directions for it. Most heartening of all, he *really* likes what he likes. His empathy and interest made telling Daphne du Maurier's story—and mine as I lived with her over many years—a challenge and a joy.

This book about a legacy owes most to my guide and friend Carolyn Heilbrun, to whom it is dedicated, and who has always known everything about women's official, subterranean, and imagined lives.

Index